MUTUAL FUND SIMPLIFIED

Answers to 101 Key Questions

Everything You Need to Know to Invest Confidently in Mutual Funds

VIVEK KUMAR BAJAJ

GUIDED SELF PUBLISHING (I)
WE CRAFT YOUR DREAMS

MUTUAL FUND SIMPLIFIED
1st Edition

Publication Date: JAN 2025
ISBN 978-93-94808-86-7

Published By
Guided Self Publishing India LLP
Sohna Gurgaon

Table of contents

About The Author ***9***

Preface ***11***

Introduction ***13***

1. What are mutual funds, and why should you invest in them? *13*

2. How is this book structured to help you? *14*

3. Who can benefit from mutual funds? *15*

4. What are the primary benefits of understanding mutual funds? *17*

5. Why are mutual funds essential for wealth creation? . *19*

Section 1: Mutual Fund Basics (Q6–Q20) ***22***

6. How do mutual funds work? *22*

7. What is the role of fund managers? *23*

8. How are mutual funds different from stocks? *25*

9. What are open-ended and closed-ended funds? *27*

10. What is the Net Asset Value (NAV)? *28*

11. What are equity mutual funds? *30*

12. What are debt mutual funds? *31*

13. What are hybrid mutual funds? *33*

14. What are sectoral and thematic funds? *34*

15. How do international mutual funds work? *36*

16. What are expense ratios? *38*

17. What are entry loads and exit loads? 39

18. How do fees impact my returns? 41

19. Are there any hidden charges in mutual funds? 42

20. How do direct plans differ from regular plans? 44

Section 2: Starting Your Investment Journey (Q21–Q40) **46**

21. How do I start investing in mutual funds? 46

22. What is KYC, and how do I complete it? 47

23. Can I invest in mutual funds without a demat account? 49

24. How much money is needed to start investing? 50

25. Can minors invest in mutual funds? 51

26. How do I select a mutual fund for my financial goals? 53

27. What are large-cap, mid-cap, and small-cap funds? . 54

28. What is a fund's objective, and why is it important? . 56

29. How to check the track record of a mutual fund? 58

30. Are past returns a reliable indicator of future performance? 59

31. What are the risks involved in mutual funds? 61

32. How do I assess my risk tolerance? 63

33. Are mutual funds less risky than stocks? 64

34. What is the risk-return trade-off? 66

35. How do diversification and asset allocation reduce risk? 67

36. Can mutual funds be used for retirement planning? . 69

37. How do I invest for short-term financial goals? 71

38. Which funds are best for children's education? 72

39. Can mutual funds generate a steady income? 74

40. What is an ELSS fund, and how does it help with taxes? 75

Section 3: Managing Your Investments (Q41–Q65) **78**

41. What is a Systematic Investment Plan (SIP)? 78

42. How does SIP work? 79

43. What is better: SIP or lump sum investment? 81

44. How to calculate SIP returns? 82

45. Can I pause or stop a SIP? 84

46. How often should I review my mutual fund portfolio? 85

47. What should I do if my mutual fund underperforms? 87

48. How to switch between mutual funds? 88

49. Can I invest in multiple mutual funds? 90

50. How to rebalance my mutual fund portfolio? 91

51. When should I redeem my mutual fund investments? 93

52. What is an exit load, and how does it affect withdrawals? 94

53. Can I partially withdraw from a mutual fund? 95

54. What are the tax implications of redeeming mutual funds? 97

55. How to transfer mutual funds to another person? 99

56. Are mutual fund returns taxable? 100

57. What is LTCG (Long-Term Capital Gains) tax? 102

58. How does STCG (Short-Term Capital Gains) tax work? 103

59. What is a tax-saving mutual fund? 105

60. How to report mutual fund gains in tax returns? 107

61. What are mutual fund investment platforms? 108

62. How does FundzBazar help simplify investments? .. 110

63. Are robo-advisors helpful for mutual fund investments? 113

64. Can I invest in mutual funds through mobile apps? 114

65. How to compare mutual funds online? 116

Section 4: Advanced Topics and Myths (Q66–Q95) 118

66. What is a fund benchmark? 118

67. How to interpret fund fact sheets? 119

68. What is the Sharpe ratio? 121

69. What is alpha and beta in mutual fund analysis? 122

70. How do index funds differ from actively managed funds? 124

71. Are mutual funds only for wealthy investors? 126

72. Do mutual funds guarantee returns? 127

73. Is it better to invest only during market lows? 129

74. Are mutual funds risk-free? 130

75. Can mutual funds make you rich quickly? 132

76. Can mutual funds invest in gold? *133*

77. What are exchange-traded funds (ETFs)? *135*

78. What is a dividend payout option in mutual funds? *136*

79. Can mutual funds invest in real estate? *138*

80. What are liquid funds? *140*

81. Can I lose all my money in a mutual fund? *141*

82. How to avoid fraud in mutual fund investments? *143*

83. How do market conditions affect mutual funds? *144*

84. Are mutual funds good for emergency funds? *146*

85. Can I hold mutual funds jointly with someone? *147*

86. What is the ideal time horizon for mutual funds? ... *149*

87. How to set realistic investment goals? *150*

88. What are the red flags to avoid in a mutual fund? .. *152*

89. Should I consider global mutual funds? *154*

90. How do I stay updated on mutual fund trends? *155*

91. How to use mutual funds for long-term wealth creation? *157*

92. What are the benefits of compounding in mutual funds? *159*

93. How to create a balanced mutual fund portfolio? ... *160*

94. What are the best practices for SIP investments? *162*

95. How to manage market volatility as a mutual fund investor? *164*

Conclusion ***166***

96. What are the key takeaways from this book? *166*

97. How to stay disciplined as a mutual fund investor? 167

98. Why should you seek professional advice when needed? *169*

99. What additional resources can help in mutual fund investing? *171*

100. How to ensure financial independence using mutual funds? *173*

101. Why is understanding mutual funds a lifelong skill? *174*

***Recap of Key Takeaways* 177**

***Final Thoughts* 179**

About The Author

Vivek Kumar Bajaj is a distinguished author and financial expert with a rich experience spanning over 22 years in the field of Mutual Fund Distribution (MFD) and investment consultancy. Throughout his career, he has dedicated himself to educating and empowering investors to make informed financial decisions.

Bajaj is not only an accomplished writer but also a passionate advocate for investor awareness. He conducts a multitude of programs aimed at educating individuals about the nuances of investments, risk management, and financial planning. His unwavering commitment to the cause of investor awareness has earned him recognition and respect in the financial industry.

As a best-selling author, Vivek Kumar Bajaj has penned numerous books that simplify complex financial concepts, making them accessible to a wide audience. His writings serve as invaluable resources for both novice and seasoned investors, enabling them to navigate the world of finance with confidence.

Beyond his professional pursuits, Vivek Kumar Bajaj enjoys a range of personal interests. He is an avid reader, constantly seeking knowledge and insights to enhance his expertise. His love for driving takes him on journeys both literal and metaphorical, as he continues to explore new horizons in the world of finance. Bajaj is also an enthusiastic campaigner, actively working to foster a society where individuals are not only aware of their investment options but are also equipped to make sound financial decisions.

In summary, Vivek Kumar Bajaj is a multifaceted individual with a wealth of experience in the financial realm. His dedication to investor awareness and his ability to communicate complex financial concepts in a relatable manner make him a prominent figure in the field of finance and investment education.

Preface

"An investment in knowledge pays the best interest."
— Benjamin Franklin

Mutual funds are no longer the mystery they once were. They have become an integral part of modern investment portfolios, offering individuals the chance to build wealth, achieve financial goals, and secure their future. Yet, for many, the world of mutual funds remains riddled with questions.

This book, Mutual Funds Simplified: Answers to 101 Key Questions, was born out of a simple idea—to provide clarity and confidence to investors, regardless of their experience. Whether you are a first-time investor wondering how to start or an experienced one seeking to refine your strategy, this book is for you.

"The stock market is filled with individuals who know the price of everything, but the value of nothing."
— Philip Fisher

Mutual funds bridge the gap between understanding value and achieving it. They offer a way for individuals to harness the potential of financial markets without needing expert-level knowledge. But to make informed decisions, you need to ask the right questions and understand the answers.

Through this book, I aim to guide you with insights into mutual funds—what they are, how they work, and how you can use them to your advantage. The questions in this book are designed to address the concerns of every investor, from the most basic to the most intricate.

"It's not about timing the market; it's about time in the market."
— Warren Buffett

Investing in mutual funds is a journey of patience, discipline, and learning. The goal of this book is to simplify the complex and inspire confidence in every reader to embark on or refine their mutual fund journey. Each question answered in these pages is a step toward making investing less daunting and more rewarding.

Thank you for picking up this book. I hope it equips you with the knowledge and tools to make smarter decisions and achieve your financial aspirations.

Warm regards,
VIVEK KUMAR BAJAJ

Introduction

1. What are mutual funds, and why should you invest in them?

Mutual funds are investment vehicles that pool money from multiple investors to purchase a diversified portfolio of stocks, bonds, or other securities. Each investor buys shares in the mutual fund, allowing them to participate in the potential growth of the fund's assets without needing to manage individual investments. Managed by professional portfolio managers, mutual funds are designed to meet various investment objectives, ranging from aggressive growth to conservative income generation. This structure offers individual investors access to diversified portfolios that they may not be able to achieve on their own due to limited capital or expertise.

One of the primary reasons to invest in mutual funds is diversification. By investing in a mutual fund, investors gain exposure to a wide range of securities, which helps spread risk. If one stock or bond performs poorly, the overall impact on the investment is mitigated by the performance of other assets in the fund. This built-in diversification is particularly beneficial for retail investors who may not have the resources to construct a similarly diversified portfolio independently. It reduces the likelihood of significant losses from a single investment and contributes to more stable long-term returns.

Another key advantage of mutual funds is professional management. Fund managers are typically experienced investment professionals who conduct extensive research and analysis to make informed investment decisions. They monitor market trends, economic indicators, and the performance of individual securities to optimize the fund's portfolio. For retail investors who may lack the time or expertise to manage their investments actively, mutual funds offer a convenient solution. Investors can benefit from the knowledge and strategies employed by seasoned professionals, increasing the potential for better financial outcomes.

Mutual funds also provide liquidity, allowing investors to buy and sell shares easily. Most mutual funds offer daily trading, meaning investors can enter or exit their positions at the end of each trading day at the fund's net asset value (NAV). This feature contrasts with certain other investment options, such as real estate or some types of bonds, which can be more challenging to liquidate. The ability to access funds quickly can be an essential factor for retail investors who may need to respond to changing financial situations.

Finally, mutual funds cater to a wide range of investment goals and risk tolerances. They come in various types and styles, including equity, fixed income, balanced, and index funds, each designed to meet specific investor needs. This variety allows retail investors to select funds aligned with their financial objectives, whether they seek growth, income, or capital preservation. By offering options that suit different risk appetites and investment horizons, mutual funds empower investors to create a personalized investment strategy that can adapt to their evolving financial circumstances.

2. How is this book structured to help you?

This book is structured to provide retail investors with a clear and accessible understanding of mutual funds through a question-and-answer format. Each chapter is designed to address specific queries that investors frequently have, making it easy to locate information relevant to your needs. By breaking down complex topics into straightforward answers, the book aims to demystify mutual funds and empower readers to make informed investment decisions.

The organization of the content follows a logical progression, starting with foundational concepts before moving into more advanced topics. This structure allows readers to build their knowledge incrementally. Each question is carefully selected to reflect common concerns and misconceptions about mutual funds, ensuring that the content is both relevant and practical. Readers can start with basic inquiries and gradually explore more nuanced discussions, facilitating a comprehensive understanding of the subject matter.

In addition to the question-and-answer format, the book includes practical examples and real-world scenarios to illustrate key points. These examples serve to contextualize the information, making it easier for retail investors to relate to and apply the concepts in their own investment strategies. By grounding theoretical information in practical applications, the book aims to enhance the reader's confidence in navigating the world of mutual funds.

Finally, the book concludes with a section dedicated to common pitfalls and best practices in mutual fund investing. This final part serves as a valuable resource for retail investors looking to avoid common mistakes and optimize their investment strategies. By providing actionable insights and advice, the book aims to equip readers with the tools necessary for successful investing, ensuring that they feel supported throughout their investment journey.

3. Who can benefit from mutual funds?

Mutual funds are designed to cater to a diverse range of investors, making them an accessible investment option for many individuals. Retail investors, who typically invest smaller amounts of money compared to institutional investors, can greatly benefit from mutual funds. These investment vehicles allow retail investors to pool their resources with others, gaining access to a professionally managed portfolio that may otherwise be unattainable for them individually. By investing in mutual funds, retail investors can diversify their holdings and mitigate risk, which is particularly important for those who may not have extensive knowledge or experience in investing.

One of the key groups that can benefit from mutual funds is novice investors. Those who are new to the world of investing may feel overwhelmed by the complexities of stock picking and market analysis. Mutual funds simplify this process by providing a ready-made portfolio managed by experienced professionals. New investors can start with relatively small amounts and gradually build their investment knowledge while benefiting from the expertise of fund managers. This educational aspect helps them become more confident and informed as they navigate their investment journey.

Additionally, busy professionals who may not have the time to actively manage their investments can find mutual funds to be an ideal solution. With demanding careers and personal commitments, many individuals lack the bandwidth to research stocks or track market trends regularly. Mutual funds allow these investors to delegate the responsibility of managing their portfolios to qualified fund managers, freeing up their time while still allowing them to participate in the financial markets. This hands-off approach can lead to better long-term investment outcomes for those who prioritize convenience.

Retirement savers also stand to gain significantly from mutual funds. Many retirement accounts, such as 401(k)s and IRAs, offer mutual fund options as part of their investment selections. These funds often provide a balanced mix of equity and fixed-income investments, helping savers build a diversified portfolio over time. By investing in mutual funds within retirement accounts, individuals can take advantage of tax benefits while working towards their long-term financial goals. This makes mutual funds a practical choice for those looking to secure their financial future during retirement.

Lastly, risk-averse investors can find mutual funds appealing due to their inherent diversification. Mutual funds typically invest in a variety of securities, which can help spread risk across different asset classes. For investors who are uncomfortable with the volatility of individual stocks or who wish to minimize their exposure to market fluctuations, mutual funds provide a balanced approach to investing. By choosing funds that align with their risk tolerance and investment objectives, these investors can pursue growth while managing the risks associated with their portfolios effectively.

4. What are the primary benefits of understanding mutual funds?

Understanding mutual funds offers several primary benefits that can significantly enhance an investor's financial acumen and decision-making capabilities. One of the foremost advantages is diversification. By pooling money with other investors, individuals can access a broader array of securities than they could on their own. This diversification reduces the risk associated with investing in a single stock or bond, as the performance of a mutual fund is less likely to be impacted by the misfortunes of any one investment. Retail investors, in particular, can benefit from this strategy, as it allows them to spread their assets across various sectors and asset classes, which can lead to more stable returns.

Another key benefit is the professional management that comes with mutual funds. These funds are typically overseen by experienced portfolio managers who have the expertise to analyze market trends and select investments accordingly. For retail investors who may not have the time or knowledge to manage their investments actively, this professional guidance can be invaluable. The managers continuously monitor the fund's performance and make necessary adjustments to the portfolio, which can lead to better outcomes than if an individual were to manage their investments independently.

Cost efficiency is also a significant advantage of understanding mutual funds. While there are fees associated with mutual funds, they often provide a more economical way to invest compared to building a diversified portfolio of individual securities. Retail investors can benefit from economies of scale, as mutual funds can negotiate lower trading costs and access investment opportunities that might be out of reach for individual investors. Understanding these costs and how they impact overall returns is essential for anyone looking to maximize their investment strategy.

Additionally, mutual funds offer liquidity, allowing investors to buy or sell shares easily. This liquidity provides retail investors with the flexibility to access their money when needed, without the complexities that can arise from selling individual stocks or bonds. Knowing how to navigate this aspect of mutual funds can empower investors to manage their finances effectively, ensuring that they can respond to changes in their financial situation or market conditions without significant delays.

Finally, understanding mutual funds can help retail investors set and achieve their financial goals more effectively. By recognizing the various types of mutual funds available—such as equity, fixed-income, or balanced funds—investors can align their choices with their risk tolerance and investment objectives. This alignment fosters a more strategic approach to investing, allowing individuals to work towards specific milestones, whether that's saving for retirement, funding education, or building wealth over time. With the right knowledge, retail investors can leverage mutual funds to create a robust investment portfolio that suits their needs and aspirations.

5. Why are mutual funds essential for wealth creation?

Mutual funds play a crucial role in wealth creation for retail investors due to their inherent structure and benefits. By pooling money from multiple investors, mutual funds provide the opportunity to invest in a diversified portfolio of assets, which reduces risk compared to investing in individual stocks or bonds. This diversification is essential because it helps to mitigate the impact of market volatility on an investor's overall portfolio. Retail investors often lack the resources or expertise to create a well-diversified investment strategy on their own, making mutual funds an attractive option for those looking to build wealth over time.

One of the significant advantages of mutual funds is their accessibility. Retail investors can start investing with relatively small amounts of money, allowing them to enter the investment world without needing a large capital base. Many mutual funds offer low minimum investment requirements, making it possible for individuals to begin their investment journey regardless of their financial situation. Additionally, mutual funds are managed by professional fund managers who conduct thorough research and analysis, enabling investors to benefit from their expertise without needing to actively manage their investments.

Cost efficiency is another essential aspect of mutual funds that contributes to wealth creation. While there are fees associated with mutual funds, such as expense ratios and management fees, these costs are often lower than those associated with managing a portfolio of individual securities. Mutual funds can achieve economies of scale, which allows them to reduce trading costs and other expenses. For retail investors, this means they can enjoy a more affordable investment option that still provides the potential for significant returns over time.

Moreover, mutual funds are designed to align with various investment goals and risk tolerances. They come in various types, including equity funds, bond funds, index funds, and balanced funds, each catering to different investment strategies. Retail investors can choose funds that match their specific objectives, whether they are seeking growth, income, or capital preservation. This ability to select funds based on personal financial goals empowers investors to take control of their wealth-building journey while also managing risk effectively.

Finally, the long-term performance of mutual funds has been historically strong, making them a reliable choice for wealth creation. Many mutual funds aim to outperform benchmarks and offer investors the potential for capital appreciation over extended periods. By regularly investing in mutual funds and taking advantage of dollar-cost averaging, retail investors can benefit from compounding returns. This strategy, combined with the advantages of diversification, professional management, and accessibility, underscores why mutual funds are essential for those looking to build and sustain wealth over time.

Section 1: Mutual Fund Basics (Q6–Q20)

6. How do mutual funds work?

Mutual funds operate as collective investment vehicles that pool money from multiple investors to purchase a diversified portfolio of stocks, bonds, or other securities. When you invest in a mutual fund, you are buying shares of the fund, which in turn owns a variety of assets. This pooling of resources allows individual investors to access a diversified portfolio that they might not be able to build on their own due to financial or logistical constraints. The fund is managed by professional investment managers who make decisions about which securities to buy and sell, aiming to achieve the fund's investment objectives.

The functioning of mutual funds is based on the concept of shared risk and reward. By investing in a mutual fund, you are not only spreading your investment across various assets, but you are also sharing the risk associated with those investments with other shareholders. This diversification can help mitigate the impact of poor performance in any single investment, as the gains from other assets can offset losses. Additionally, mutual funds offer various types of investments, including equity funds, bond funds, and balanced funds, catering to different risk appetites and investment goals.

Investors typically buy and sell mutual fund shares at the net asset value (NAV), which is calculated at the end of each trading day. The NAV is determined by taking the total value of the fund's assets, subtracting any liabilities, and dividing by the number of outstanding shares. This daily valuation means that investors know exactly what their shares are worth at the close of the market. When you decide to invest in a mutual fund, your purchase price is based on the NAV at the end of the trading day when your order is executed, while selling your shares is also done at the NAV, ensuring transparency in pricing.

Mutual funds charge fees for their management and operational services, which can impact overall returns. These fees can include management fees, which compensate the fund manager for their expertise and time, and other costs such as administrative expenses. Some funds may also charge sales loads, which are fees paid when buying or selling shares. It is crucial for investors to understand these costs as they can vary significantly between funds and can erode returns over time. Many funds provide a breakdown of their fees in their prospectus, making it essential to review this document before investing.

Finally, mutual funds are subject to regulatory oversight, which adds a layer of protection for investors. In the United States, the Securities and Exchange Commission (SEC) regulates mutual funds, requiring them to provide detailed information about their investments, fees, and performance. This regulatory framework helps ensure transparency and helps investors make informed decisions. For retail investors looking to enter the world of investing, understanding how mutual funds work is a vital step towards building a diversified investment portfolio that aligns with their financial goals.

7. What is the role of fund managers?

Fund managers play a crucial role in the investment landscape, particularly for retail investors who may not have the time or expertise to manage their portfolios effectively. These professionals are responsible for making investment decisions on behalf of mutual fund shareholders. Their primary objective is to maximize returns while managing risk, which involves selecting securities that align with the fund's investment strategy and objectives. Fund managers conduct extensive research and analysis to identify potential investments, monitor market conditions, and adjust their strategies as needed to respond to changing economic environments.

One of the key responsibilities of fund managers is asset allocation. This refers to the process of dividing the fund's investments among different asset classes, such as stocks, bonds, and cash equivalents. A well-thought-out asset allocation strategy can help mitigate risks and enhance overall returns. Fund managers use various tools and methodologies to determine the optimal allocation that aligns with the fund's goals and the risk tolerance of its investors. This requires not only a deep understanding of market trends and economic indicators but also the ability to forecast how different assets will perform in various scenarios.

In addition to asset allocation, fund managers are tasked with security selection, which involves choosing specific securities to purchase or sell within the fund. This process requires a comprehensive evaluation of individual companies, sectors, and industries. Fund managers analyze financial statements, assess management teams, and evaluate competitive positions to identify stocks or bonds that are likely to yield strong performance. The expertise and judgment of fund managers can significantly influence a fund's returns, making their role pivotal in the investment process.

Fund managers also play a critical role in monitoring and rebalancing the portfolio. Over time, the performance of different securities can lead to shifts in the fund's asset allocation, which may deviate from the original investment strategy. To ensure that the portfolio remains aligned with its goals, fund managers regularly review its composition and make necessary adjustments. This may involve selling underperforming investments, adding new securities, or reallocating funds among asset classes. This ongoing management is vital for maintaining the intended risk-return profile of the mutual fund.

Finally, communication is an essential aspect of a fund manager's role. They are responsible for providing regular updates to investors regarding the fund's performance, investment strategy, and market outlook. This transparency helps build trust and keeps investors informed about how their money is being managed. Fund managers often produce reports, hold conference calls, and engage with investors to explain their decisions and the rationale behind them. By fostering clear communication, fund managers enhance investor confidence and ensure that retail investors feel connected to their investments.

8. How are mutual funds different from stocks?

Mutual funds and stocks represent two distinct types of investment vehicles, each with its own characteristics, advantages, and risks. Stocks represent ownership in a specific company, allowing investors to share in the company's profits and losses. When you purchase a stock, you buy a small piece of that company, and your investment's value is directly tied to its performance in the market. In contrast, mutual funds pool money from multiple investors to purchase a diversified portfolio of stocks, bonds, or other securities. This collective approach allows for diversification, which can reduce risk compared to investing in individual stocks.

One of the most significant differences between mutual funds and stocks is the level of diversification. When investing in a stock, an investor is exposed to the risks associated with that single company, such as business performance, market competition, and economic conditions. In contrast, mutual funds typically hold a variety of assets, spreading risk across multiple securities. This diversification can help mitigate losses if one particular stock underperforms, as the positive performance of other investments in the fund can offset some of the negative impacts.

Another key difference lies in management. Stocks are generally self-managed investments, requiring investors to actively monitor and make decisions based on their performance. This can involve researching company fundamentals, market trends, and economic indicators. Mutual funds, however, are managed by professional fund managers who make investment decisions on behalf of the investors. These professionals analyze market conditions, select securities, and continuously adjust the portfolio to meet the fund's investment objectives. This professional management can be particularly beneficial for retail investors who may not have the time or expertise to manage their investments actively.

Liquidity also varies between mutual funds and stocks. Stocks can be bought and sold at any time during market hours, providing high liquidity. Investors can react quickly to market changes, buying or selling shares based on real-time information. In contrast, mutual funds are typically bought and sold at the end of the trading day at the fund's net asset value (NAV). This means that while mutual funds are still considered liquid investments, they do not offer the same immediacy as stocks, which can be a critical factor for some investors.

Lastly, the cost structure differs significantly between the two. Investing in stocks generally incurs brokerage commissions and potentially capital gains taxes when shares are sold for a profit. Mutual funds, on the other hand, may charge management fees, sales loads, and other expenses that can impact overall returns. While some mutual funds are designed to be low-cost and passively managed (like index funds), others may have higher fees due to active management strategies. Understanding these cost implications is essential for investors when deciding between mutual funds and stocks, as it can influence overall investment performance.

9. What are open-ended and closed-ended funds?

Open-ended and closed-ended funds are two primary types of mutual funds that cater to different investment needs and strategies. Open-ended funds are investment vehicles that allow investors to buy and sell shares at any time, directly from the fund company. These funds do not have a fixed number of shares; instead, they continuously issue new shares as investors invest and redeem shares when investors withdraw their money. This flexibility makes open-ended funds particularly appealing to retail investors seeking liquidity and ease of access to their investments.

In contrast, closed-ended funds operate differently. They issue a fixed number of shares through an initial public offering (IPO) and subsequently trade on stock exchanges like individual stocks. Once the shares are issued, the fund does not create new shares or redeem existing ones. Instead, the market determines the price of the shares based on supply and demand. This structure can lead to scenarios where closed-ended fund shares trade at a premium or discount to their net asset value (NAV), adding an additional layer of complexity for investors.

The pricing mechanisms of these two types of funds are a key differentiator. Open-ended funds are priced once a day at the end of the trading day, with the NAV reflecting the total value of the fund's assets divided by the number of outstanding shares. Closed-ended funds, however, can fluctuate throughout the trading day, with prices influenced by market sentiment, investor demand, and broader market conditions. This can sometimes create opportunities for savvy investors to purchase closed-ended fund shares at a discount to their underlying assets.

Another important distinction lies in the investment strategies employed by these funds. Open-ended funds often focus on long-term growth and provide investors with a diversified portfolio managed by professionals. They tend to be more suitable for retail investors who prefer a buy-and-hold strategy, allowing for gradual wealth accumulation over time. Closed-ended funds, on the other hand, may employ more aggressive strategies, including leveraging and investing in niche markets, which can lead to higher potential returns but also greater risks.

Both open-ended and closed-ended funds play vital roles in the investment landscape, each catering to different investor profiles and objectives. Understanding the fundamental differences between these fund types empowers retail investors to make informed decisions based on their individual financial goals, risk tolerance, and investment horizons. By recognizing the unique features of each, investors can better navigate the growing array of mutual fund options available in today's market.

10. What is the Net Asset Value (NAV)?

Net Asset Value (NAV) is a crucial concept for retail investors, particularly when dealing with mutual funds. It represents the per-share value of a mutual fund, calculated by taking the total value of the fund's assets, subtracting its liabilities, and then dividing that amount by the total number of outstanding shares. This figure is vital for investors as it helps them understand the current worth of their investment in the fund. NAV is typically calculated at the end of each trading day, reflecting the closing prices of the securities held within the fund.

The significance of NAV lies in its role as a benchmark for buying and selling mutual fund shares. When investors purchase shares of a mutual fund, they do so at the fund's NAV at the end of the trading day, which is known as the purchase price. Conversely, when investors decide to redeem their shares, they receive the NAV as the selling price. This transparent pricing mechanism allows investors to gauge the performance of their investments over time and make informed decisions about their asset allocation.

Investors should also be aware that NAV does not account for any sales loads or fees associated with the mutual fund. These additional costs can affect the overall return on investment and should be considered when evaluating a fund's attractiveness. It's essential to look beyond the NAV itself and examine the total expense ratio, which encompasses all fees and expenses relative to the fund's assets. This comprehensive view enables investors to understand the real costs of investing in a particular mutual fund.

Fluctuations in NAV can occur due to changes in the market value of the underlying assets, thus influencing the fund's performance. For example, if the stocks or bonds within a fund appreciate in value, the NAV will increase, reflecting this growth. Conversely, if the market takes a downturn, the NAV may decline, indicating a loss in asset value. These movements can impact investor sentiment and decisions, underscoring the importance of staying informed about market conditions and the specific assets held within the fund.

Finally, while NAV is a fundamental metric for assessing mutual fund performance, it should not be the sole criterion for investment decisions. Retail investors should consider other factors such as the fund's historical performance, investment strategy, risk profile, and management team. By taking a holistic approach to evaluating mutual funds, investors can make more informed choices that align with their financial goals and risk tolerance, ultimately leading to a more successful investing experience.

11. What are equity mutual funds?

Equity mutual funds are investment vehicles that pool money from multiple investors to purchase a diversified portfolio of stocks. These funds aim to provide capital appreciation over time, making them a popular choice for retail investors seeking long-term growth. By investing in a variety of companies across different sectors, equity mutual funds can help mitigate the risks associated with investing in individual stocks. This diversification is key to achieving a more stable return, as the performance of one stock can be offset by the performance of others within the fund.

There are different types of equity mutual funds, categorized based on their investment strategy, market capitalization, and investment style. For instance, large-cap equity funds focus on well-established companies with a significant market presence, while small-cap funds target smaller, potentially high-growth firms. Additionally, equity funds can be actively managed, where fund managers make decisions on stock selection, or passively managed, where funds aim to replicate the performance of a specific index.

This variety allows investors to choose funds that align with their risk tolerance and investment goals.

One of the primary advantages of equity mutual funds is their potential for high returns, particularly over the long term. Historically, equity markets have outperformed other asset classes like bonds and cash equivalents. However, investors should also be aware of the inherent volatility associated with stock markets. While equity mutual funds can provide significant growth opportunities, they are subject to market fluctuations, which can lead to short-term losses. Understanding this risk is essential for retail investors as they navigate their investment choices.

Investors in equity mutual funds should also consider the fees associated with these funds. Management fees, expense ratios, and other costs can impact overall returns. Actively managed funds typically have higher fees compared to passive funds due to the active management strategy employed. It is crucial for retail investors to evaluate these costs in conjunction with the fund's historical performance and investment strategy to determine whether the fund is a suitable investment for their portfolio.

In summary, equity mutual funds offer a practical way for retail investors to participate in the stock market while benefiting from professional management and diversification. By understanding the various types of equity funds, their potential for returns, associated risks, and costs, investors can make informed decisions that align with their financial objectives. As with any investment, it is essential to conduct thorough research and consider personal risk tolerance before committing funds to equity mutual funds.

12. What are debt mutual funds?

Debt mutual funds are investment vehicles that primarily invest in fixed-income securities such as government bonds, corporate bonds, and other debt instruments. Retail investors often find these funds appealing due to their potential for stable returns compared to equity mutual funds. The primary objective of debt mutual funds is to provide investors with regular income while preserving capital. By pooling money from various investors, these funds are able to diversify their investments across different types of debt instruments, thereby reducing the risk associated with individual securities.

One of the key advantages of debt mutual funds is their relatively lower risk profile. Unlike equity markets, which can experience significant volatility, debt instruments typically offer more predictable returns. This stability makes debt mutual funds an attractive option for conservative investors or those looking for a steady income stream. Additionally, these funds are managed by professional fund managers who analyze the creditworthiness of issuers and interest rate trends, which can enhance the chances of achieving better returns for investors.

Debt mutual funds are categorized based on the maturity of the underlying securities they invest in. Short-term funds invest in instruments with shorter maturities, typically up to three years, while long-term funds invest in securities with longer durations. There are also other categories, such as dynamic bond funds, which adjust their portfolio based on interest rate movements. Understanding these categories can help retail investors choose the right type of debt mutual fund based on their investment horizon and risk appetite.

Investors should also be aware of the tax implications associated with debt mutual funds. The taxation of income from these funds can differ based on the holding period. If held for more than three years, gains from debt mutual funds are taxed at a lower long-term capital gains tax rate, which can be beneficial for investors looking for tax-efficient investment options. This aspect can make debt mutual funds an appealing choice for those who want to grow their wealth while managing tax liabilities.

In conclusion, debt mutual funds serve as a viable investment option for retail investors seeking stability and regular income. With their lower risk profile, professional management, and potential tax advantages, these funds can play a crucial role in a diversified investment portfolio. By understanding the various types of debt mutual funds and their characteristics, investors can make informed decisions that align with their financial goals and risk tolerance.

13. What are hybrid mutual funds?

Hybrid mutual funds are investment vehicles that combine elements of both equity and debt instruments. This dual approach allows investors to benefit from the potential high returns associated with equities while also enjoying the stability and lower risk typically associated with fixed-income securities. Hybrid funds are designed to cater to a range of risk appetites, making them an attractive option for retail investors looking for a balanced investment strategy.

There are various types of hybrid mutual funds, each designed to meet specific investment objectives. For instance, balanced funds maintain a relatively equal allocation between stocks and bonds, aiming to provide moderate growth and income. Conversely, aggressive hybrid funds may tilt more heavily towards equities, seeking higher returns but with increased risk. On the other hand, conservative hybrid funds lean towards fixed-income securities to prioritize capital preservation and steady income, appealing to risk-averse investors.

The flexibility of hybrid mutual funds allows fund managers to adjust the allocation between equity and debt based on market conditions. This tactical adjustment can potentially enhance returns while managing risk effectively. For example, during bullish market periods, managers may increase equity exposure to capitalize on rising stock prices. Conversely, in bearish markets, they may shift towards bonds to safeguard the portfolio from volatility. This adaptability makes hybrid funds particularly appealing for investors who wish to navigate varying economic climates without needing to actively manage their investments.

Investors should also consider the costs associated with hybrid mutual funds. Like all mutual funds, these funds charge management fees and sometimes have sales loads. It is essential for retail investors to scrutinize these fees, as they can significantly impact overall returns over time. Additionally, understanding the fund's investment strategy, risk profile, and historical performance is crucial for making informed investment decisions. Reading the fund's prospectus can provide valuable insights into how the fund operates and the risks involved.

In summary, hybrid mutual funds offer a versatile investment option for retail investors seeking a balanced approach to their portfolios. By blending equity and debt instruments, these funds can provide an efficient way to achieve growth while managing risk. As with any investment, it is important for investors to thoroughly research and understand the specific hybrid fund they are considering, ensuring it aligns with their financial goals and risk tolerance.

14. What are sectoral and thematic funds?

Sectoral and thematic funds are specialized types of mutual funds that focus on specific sectors of the economy or particular investment themes. These funds allow investors to target their investments based on prevailing economic trends or sectors they believe will perform well in the future. Unlike diversified funds that spread their investments across various sectors to mitigate risk, sectoral and thematic funds concentrate their holdings in a limited number of companies, which can lead to higher potential returns but also comes with increased risk.

Sectoral funds invest exclusively in companies operating within a particular industry sector, such as technology, healthcare, or energy. By doing so, they aim to capitalize on the growth potential of that sector. For instance, a technology sector fund would invest in companies involved in software development, hardware manufacturing, or information technology services. Investors who have confidence in a sector's growth trajectory may find these funds appealing as they offer the chance to benefit directly from sector-specific trends.

Thematic funds, on the other hand, are built around broader investment themes that may cut across various sectors. These themes can be based on macroeconomic trends, demographic shifts, or emerging technologies. For example, a fund focusing on renewable energy might invest in companies across sectors such as solar power, wind energy, and energy storage. Thematic funds allow investors to tap into trends that they believe will shape the future economy, providing an opportunity for capitalizing on longer-term growth prospects.

Both sectoral and thematic funds can be more volatile than traditional mutual funds due to their concentrated nature. This focus can lead to significant gains if the targeted sector or theme performs well; however, it also increases the risk of losses if those sectors face downturns. Retail investors should carefully consider their risk tolerance and investment horizon before investing in these funds. Diversification can be a key strategy to manage risk, and investors may want to balance sectoral or thematic investments with more diversified options.

Investors interested in sectoral and thematic funds should conduct thorough research to understand the underlying factors driving the sectors or themes they wish to invest in. It is essential to analyze market trends, economic indicators, and specific company performances within those sectors. Additionally, investors should pay attention to the fund manager's expertise and track record in managing sectoral or thematic investments, as this can significantly impact the fund's performance. By gaining a deeper understanding of these specialized funds, retail investors can make informed decisions that align with their investment objectives.

15. How do international mutual funds work?

International mutual funds are investment vehicles that pool money from multiple investors to purchase a diversified portfolio of assets located outside the investor's home country. These funds provide retail investors with an opportunity to gain exposure to foreign markets, economies, and currencies without the need to invest directly in individual foreign stocks or bonds. By utilizing the expertise of professional fund managers, investors can benefit from diversified portfolios that are designed to capitalize on growth opportunities globally.

The operation of international mutual funds begins with the fund manager, who conducts extensive research to identify attractive investment opportunities across various countries. This research includes analyzing economic indicators, political stability, market trends, and company performance within the targeted regions. Once the investment strategy is defined, the fund manager allocates the pooled capital into a mix of equities, fixed income securities, and other assets that are expected to provide returns over the long term. This strategic allocation is critical in managing risks associated with currency fluctuations and geopolitical events.

Investors in international mutual funds typically buy shares in the fund, which represent a proportional stake in the underlying assets. The price of these shares, known as the net asset value (NAV), fluctuates based on the market value of the fund's holdings. Investors may purchase shares directly from the fund company or through a financial advisor. Additionally, international mutual funds are subject to various fees, including management fees and operating expenses, which can affect overall returns. Understanding these costs is essential for retail investors seeking to maximize their investment outcomes.

One of the key benefits of international mutual funds is diversification. By investing in a variety of foreign markets and sectors, investors can reduce the overall risk associated with their investment portfolios. This diversification helps to mitigate the impact of negative economic events in any single country or region. Furthermore, international mutual funds can provide access to emerging markets that may offer higher growth potential compared to more established economies, allowing investors to capitalize on global economic trends.

Retail investors should also be aware of the potential risks associated with international mutual funds. These include currency risk, where fluctuations in exchange rates can affect the value of investments; political risk, which pertains to instability in foreign governments; and market risk, which reflects the volatility of foreign markets. Investors are encouraged to evaluate their risk tolerance and investment objectives carefully before committing to international mutual funds. By doing so, they can make informed decisions that align with their financial goals while benefiting from the opportunities presented by global investing.

16. What are expense ratios?

Expense ratios are a critical aspect of mutual funds that retail investors need to understand. An expense ratio is a measure of the costs associated with managing a mutual fund, expressed as a percentage of the fund's average assets under management. This ratio includes various expenses such as management fees, administrative costs, and other operational expenses. By understanding the expense ratio, investors can gauge how much of their investment returns may be impacted by these costs.

The calculation of the expense ratio typically involves dividing the total expenses of the fund by the average value of the fund's assets over a specific period, usually a year. For example, if a mutual fund has total expenses of $1 million and average assets of $100 million, the expense ratio would be 1%. This means that for every dollar invested in the fund, 1 cent goes toward covering the fund's expenses. It is important for investors to recognize that a higher expense ratio can significantly erode returns over time, especially in the context of long-term investments.

Expense ratios can vary widely among mutual funds. Actively managed funds tend to have higher expense ratios compared to passively managed funds, such as index funds. This difference arises because actively managed funds involve more resources and management efforts to select securities, which results in higher fees. On the other hand, index funds aim to replicate the performance of a specific market index and typically have lower operating costs. Retail investors should compare the expense ratios of similar funds to make informed decisions about where to allocate their investments.

When evaluating expense ratios, it is also essential to consider the fund's performance in relation to its costs. A fund with a low expense ratio may not always be the best choice if it consistently underperforms its benchmark. Conversely, a fund with a higher expense ratio may justify its costs through superior performance. Therefore, investors should analyze both the expense ratio and the fund's historical performance to assess whether the fees are commensurate with the returns generated.

In conclusion, understanding expense ratios is crucial for retail investors looking to maximize their investment returns. By carefully evaluating the costs associated with mutual funds, investors can make more informed choices that align with their financial goals. It is advisable to seek a balance between reasonable expense ratios and solid fund performance, ensuring that they are not only aware of the costs but also the value being provided in return for those costs.

17. What are entry loads and exit loads?

Entry loads and exit loads are terms commonly used in the context of mutual funds, referring to the fees associated with buying into or selling out of a fund. An entry load is a fee charged to investors when they purchase shares of a mutual fund. This fee is typically expressed as a percentage of the amount invested and is deducted from the initial investment amount. For instance, if an investor puts in $1,000 into a fund with a 2% entry load, $20 will be taken as a fee, and only $980 will be invested in the fund. These charges are designed to cover the costs associated with the fund's marketing and distribution efforts.

On the other hand, exit loads are fees incurred when investors choose to redeem their shares or withdraw funds from a mutual fund. Similar to entry loads, exit loads are also expressed as a percentage of the redemption amount. For example, if an investor redeems $1,000 from a fund with a 1% exit load, they would receive only $990 after the fee is deducted. Exit loads may vary depending on how long the investor has held the fund; many funds impose higher exit loads for redemptions made within a short period, thereby encouraging investors to maintain their investment for a longer duration.

Investors should be aware that both entry and exit loads can impact overall returns. When evaluating mutual funds, it is essential to consider these fees in conjunction with the fund’s performance and expense ratio. While some investors may be willing to pay entry loads for funds that have a strong track record of performance, others may prefer no-load funds, which do not charge either entry or exit fees. No-load funds can be particularly appealing to retail investors, as they allow for more straightforward investment without the additional costs that can erode returns.

Regulatory changes have influenced the prevalence of entry and exit loads in the mutual fund industry. Many countries have shifted towards a no-load model, encouraging fund companies to offer products without these fees. This trend has made it easier for retail investors to access funds without incurring high costs upfront or when redeeming their investments. However, it’s crucial for investors to read the fund's prospectus carefully and understand the fee structure before committing their capital.

In summary, entry loads and exit loads are important considerations for retail investors looking to invest in mutual funds. These fees can significantly affect the net returns of an investment over time. Understanding how these charges work, along with the potential impact on investment performance, will enable investors to make more informed decisions and choose funds that align with their financial goals while minimizing unnecessary costs.

18. How do fees impact my returns?

Fees are an inevitable aspect of investing in mutual funds, and understanding their impact on returns is crucial for retail investors. Mutual funds typically charge various fees, including management fees, expense ratios, and sales loads. These fees are intended to cover the costs associated with managing the fund and providing investors with services. However, they can significantly erode an investor's returns over time. It is essential to recognize that even seemingly small fees can compound and lead to substantial losses in potential earnings.

One of the primary fees associated with mutual funds is the expense ratio, which is the percentage of the fund's assets used for operational expenses. This ratio includes management fees, administrative costs, and other fees incurred during the fund's operation. A higher expense ratio means that a larger portion of your investment is being consumed by fees, which ultimately reduces your overall returns. Retail investors should carefully compare the expense ratios of different funds before making investment decisions, as even a difference of 1% can have a considerable impact over the long term.

Sales loads are another fee that can affect investment returns. These are charges assessed when buying or selling mutual fund shares, typically expressed as a percentage of the investment amount. Front-end loads are charged at the time of purchase, while back-end loads are charged when shares are sold. These fees can deter investors from making trades, as they reduce the amount of capital working for them. Retail investors should consider no-load funds, which do not charge these fees, to maximize their potential returns.

In addition to these explicit fees, investors must also consider the implicit costs associated with mutual fund investments, such as trading costs. Funds that engage in frequent trading within their portfolios may incur higher transaction costs, which can detract from returns. Furthermore, the tax implications of mutual fund distributions can also impact net returns. Retail investors should be aware of a fund's turnover rate and its approach to managing capital gains, as these factors can influence overall performance.

Ultimately, the impact of fees on investment returns cannot be overstated. Retail investors should be diligent in researching and selecting mutual funds with low fees and transparent cost structures. By understanding how fees work and their effect on returns, investors can make informed choices that align with their financial goals. Prioritizing funds with lower expense ratios and minimal sales loads can significantly enhance long-term investment performance, allowing investors to retain more of their hard-earned returns.

19. Are there any hidden charges in mutual funds?

When considering mutual funds, many retail investors often overlook the potential for hidden charges that can affect their overall returns. Understanding the fee structure is crucial, as it ensures that investors are well-informed about the costs associated with their investment choices. While mutual funds may advertise low expense ratios, there are several additional fees that can significantly impact the net returns an investor receives.

One of the most common hidden charges in mutual funds is the sales load, which is a commission paid to brokers or financial advisors for selling the fund. Sales loads can be front-end, charged at the time of purchase, or back-end, deducted when shares are sold. While some funds are load-free, investors should carefully review the fee structure of any fund they consider, as these charges can range from 1% to over 5%, depending on the fund type and share class.

Another potential hidden charge is the management fee, which compensates the fund manager for their expertise in managing the fund's portfolio. While these fees are often disclosed as part of the fund's expense ratio, they can vary widely among funds. High management fees can erode returns over time, especially in a low-return environment. Retail investors should compare management fees across similar funds to ensure they are not overpaying for management services.

Additionally, investors should be aware of other operational fees that can affect their investments, such as redemption fees, exchange fees, and account maintenance fees. Redemption fees are typically charged if shares are sold within a certain period after purchase, while exchange fees may apply if investors switch between different funds within the same family. These fees can vary by fund and may not be prominently advertised, making it essential for investors to read the fund's prospectus thoroughly.

20. How do direct plans differ from regular plans?

Direct plans and regular plans are two distinct types of mutual fund investment options, each designed to cater to different investor needs and preferences. The primary difference lies in the distribution channel through which these plans are offered. Direct plans are sold directly by the mutual fund house without intermediaries, while regular plans involve a third party, typically a financial advisor or broker, who provides investment services. This fundamental distinction influences various factors such as expense ratios, investment costs, and investor control.

One of the most significant differences between direct and regular plans is the expense ratio. Direct plans usually have a lower expense ratio compared to regular plans because they do not incur distribution costs associated with intermediaries. This can lead to higher returns for investors in direct plans over the long term, as more of their money is invested rather than being used to pay commissions or fees to brokers. Retail investors should carefully consider this difference, as lower costs can significantly enhance overall investment performance.

Investors in direct plans often enjoy greater transparency and control over their investments. Because there is no intermediary involved, investors can make decisions directly with the mutual fund company and access real-time information about their investments. This direct communication can lead to a better understanding of the fund's performance and strategy, enabling investors to make informed decisions based on their financial goals. In contrast, regular plan investors may rely on their financial advisor for information and insights, potentially creating a layer of separation between them and their investments.

Another aspect to consider is the level of personalized advice provided in regular plans. Investors who prefer a hands-on approach and require guidance in their investment journey might find regular plans more suitable. Financial advisors can offer tailored advice based on an investor's risk tolerance, financial goals, and market conditions. This relationship can be beneficial for retail investors who feel overwhelmed by the complexities of mutual fund investments and seek professional assistance to navigate their options.

Ultimately, the choice between direct and regular plans depends on an investor's individual preferences and financial circumstances. Retail investors who are comfortable managing their investments independently and are focused on minimizing costs may gravitate towards direct plans. Conversely, those who value personalized advice and are willing to pay for it might prefer regular plans. Understanding these differences is crucial for making informed investment decisions that align with one's financial objectives and investment style.

Section 2: Starting Your Investment Journey (Q21–Q40)

21. How do I start investing in mutual funds?

Starting to invest in mutual funds can be a straightforward process, especially for retail investors looking to grow their wealth over time. The first step is to understand what mutual funds are and how they work. A mutual fund pools money from various investors to purchase a diversified portfolio of stocks, bonds, or other securities. Each investor buys shares in the fund, and the value of those shares fluctuates based on the performance of the underlying investments. With this foundational knowledge, you can make informed decisions about your investment strategy.

Next, it is essential to assess your financial goals and risk tolerance. Consider what you want to achieve with your investments, whether it's saving for retirement, a child's education, or a major purchase. Your time horizon will also influence your choices; longer time frames may allow for more aggressive investments, while shorter timelines often necessitate a more conservative approach. Understanding your risk tolerance will help you select mutual funds that align with your comfort level regarding market fluctuations and potential losses.

Once you have established your goals and risk profile, you can start researching different mutual funds. Look for funds that match your investment strategy, focusing on factors such as past performance, management fees, and the fund's investment objectives. It is crucial to read the fund's prospectus, which provides detailed information about its holdings, fees, and management. This document will help you understand how the fund operates and whether it fits your investment criteria.

Opening an investment account is the next step in starting your mutual fund journey. You can typically choose between a brokerage account or an account with a mutual fund company. If you opt for a brokerage account, you will have access to a variety of funds from different providers. Conversely, investing directly through a mutual fund company may offer lower fees for certain funds. Be prepared to provide personal information, including your Social Security number and financial details, as part of the account setup process.

Finally, once your account is established and you've selected the mutual funds that align with your investment goals, you can begin investing. Decide how much money you want to invest initially and whether you plan to make additional contributions over time. Many investors choose to set up automatic contributions to make investing a regular habit. Regularly review your investments to ensure they continue to meet your goals, and be prepared to make adjustments as needed based on changes in your financial situation or market conditions. By following these steps, you can confidently start your investment journey in mutual funds.

22. What is KYC, and how do I complete it?

KYC, or Know Your Customer, is a fundamental process that financial institutions, including mutual fund companies, use to verify the identity of their investors. This procedure is essential for preventing fraud, money laundering, and other illegal activities. KYC involves collecting personal information such as name, address, date of birth, and identification documents. By requiring this information, financial institutions can ensure they are dealing with legitimate investors and can provide a secure investment environment.

To complete the KYC process, retail investors need to gather specific documentation. Commonly required documents include a government-issued photo ID, such as a passport or driver's license, proof of address, such as a utility bill or bank statement, and in some cases, a photograph. Investors may need to provide their tax identification number, depending on the regulations in their country. It is crucial to ensure that all documents are current and valid to avoid delays in the investment process.

Investors can typically complete KYC in several ways. The most common method is through the mutual fund company's online portal, where investors can submit their documents digitally. Many companies also offer the option to complete KYC in person at their branches or through authorized intermediaries. Some financial institutions have embraced technology, allowing investors to complete the process using video KYC, where an agent verifies the investor's identity via a live video call.

After submitting the necessary documentation, the mutual fund company will review the information provided. This review process may take a few days, depending on the company’s policies and the volume of applications being processed. Investors can usually track the status of their KYC application through the company's online platform. Once KYC is successfully completed, investors will receive a confirmation, allowing them to proceed with their mutual fund investments.

It is essential for retail investors to understand that KYC is not a one-time process. Regulations may require periodic updates to KYC information, especially if there are significant changes in an investor's personal details or if the financial institution requests updates for compliance purposes. Staying proactive about KYC ensures that investors remain compliant with regulations and can continue to enjoy a seamless investment experience in the mutual fund space.

23. Can I invest in mutual funds without a demat account?

Investing in mutual funds typically raises questions about the necessity of a demat account. A demat account, short for a dematerialized account, is primarily used for holding shares and securities in an electronic format. However, when it comes to mutual funds, the situation is somewhat different. Retail investors can indeed invest in mutual funds without needing a demat account, as mutual funds operate under a distinct regulatory framework compared to direct stock investments.

When investing in mutual funds, investors have the option to purchase units directly from the mutual fund company or through a registered intermediary, such as a broker or a financial advisor. This process does not inherently require a demat account. Instead, mutual funds are held in a separate account known as a folio. A folio number is assigned to each investor, which helps the mutual fund house keep track of the investments made in various schemes without the need for a demat account.

For those who choose to invest in mutual funds without a demat account, the units are registered in the investor's name in the mutual fund's records. This means that the investor receives a statement of account instead of physical or dematerialized units. Additionally, mutual funds offer the convenience of SIPs (Systematic Investment Plans), which allow investors to contribute a fixed amount regularly without the complexities associated with managing a demat account.

Despite not requiring a demat account, some investors may still prefer to open one for various reasons. For instance, if an investor intends to hold both stocks and mutual funds, having a demat account can streamline the management of their overall portfolio. However, for those focusing solely on mutual funds, the folio system offers a straightforward and hassle-free approach to investing.

In conclusion, retail investors can confidently invest in mutual funds without a demat account. The process is designed to be accessible and uncomplicated, allowing individuals to start their investment journey with ease. Understanding the operational differences between mutual funds and stocks can empower investors to make informed decisions that align with their financial goals.

24. How much money is needed to start investing?

Determining how much money is needed to start investing in mutual funds depends on various factors, including individual financial goals, investment strategies, and the specific mutual funds one chooses. Many mutual funds have minimum investment requirements that can range from as low as $100 to several thousand dollars. Retail investors should carefully review these requirements before selecting a fund, as this will influence their initial investment decision.

Another important consideration is the investment horizon. Investors who plan to invest for the long term may find it beneficial to start with a larger initial investment, allowing them to take advantage of compounding returns over time.

However, those with limited funds can still make progress by starting with a smaller amount and gradually increasing their investments as their financial situation improves. The key is to establish a consistent investment habit, regardless of the initial amount.

Retail investors should also take into account their overall financial situation before deciding how much to invest. Factors such as emergency savings, debt levels, and other financial obligations play a crucial role in determining how much capital can be allocated to mutual funds. It is generally advisable to have an emergency fund in place and to avoid investing money that may be needed for immediate expenses or obligations.

Additionally, the choice of mutual fund can impact the amount needed to start investing. Some funds offer lower minimum investment thresholds, making them more accessible for retail investors. Moreover, investors may consider no-load funds, which do not charge a sales commission, allowing more of their money to be invested right away. Understanding the different types of funds available can help investors make informed decisions that align with their financial capabilities.

Finally, retail investors should remember that investing in mutual funds is not solely about the initial investment amount. Regular contributions, whether monthly or quarterly, can significantly enhance the growth of an investment portfolio over time. Setting up automatic contributions can help investors stay disciplined, allowing them to build wealth incrementally while benefiting from dollar-cost averaging, which can reduce the impact of market volatility on their investments.

25. Can minors invest in mutual funds?

Minors can indeed invest in mutual funds, but there are specific regulations and requirements that govern this process. In most cases, minors are not legally able to open investment accounts in their own names. Instead, they typically require a custodial account managed by an adult, usually a parent or guardian. This structure allows adults to oversee the investment decisions made on behalf of the minor until they reach the age of majority, which is commonly 18 or 21 years old, depending on jurisdiction.

Setting up a custodial account is a straightforward process. The adult must choose a financial institution that offers custodial accounts, often referred to as UGMA (Uniform Gifts to Minors Act) or UTMA (Uniform Transfers to Minors Act) accounts. These accounts allow the adult custodian to manage investments within them, including mutual funds, until the minor reaches the legal age. Once that age is reached, the minor gains full control over the account and can decide how to manage their investments moving forward.

Investing in mutual funds through a custodial account can be a beneficial way for minors to start their investment journey early. It provides an opportunity to learn about financial markets and the importance of long-term savings. Additionally, mutual funds can offer a diversified investment approach, which can be particularly advantageous for young investors who may not have the knowledge or resources to pick individual stocks. This diversification can help mitigate risks associated with investing.

There are also tax implications to consider when minors invest in mutual funds through custodial accounts. Generally, the income generated within these accounts is taxed under the minor's name, which can result in lower tax rates than those applicable to adults. However, it is essential to be aware of the "kiddie tax" rules, which can impose taxes on unearned income above a certain threshold at the parents' tax rate. Understanding these tax implications can help in planning the investments more effectively.

In conclusion, while minors can invest in mutual funds, doing so requires the establishment of a custodial account managed by an adult. This setup not only allows minors to gain valuable investment experience but also encourages responsible financial habits from an early age. By navigating the rules and regulations surrounding custodial accounts and considering the associated tax implications, parents can effectively guide their children in building a solid foundation for their financial futures.

26. How do I select a mutual fund for my financial goals?

Selecting a mutual fund to align with your financial goals requires a systematic approach that considers various factors tailored to your individual needs. First, it is essential to define your financial objectives. Are you saving for retirement, a child's education, or a major purchase? Each goal may require a different investment strategy, risk tolerance, and time horizon. Understanding these elements will provide a clear framework for your mutual fund selection process.

Next, assess your risk tolerance. Mutual funds come in various forms, ranging from conservative bond funds to aggressive equity funds. Knowing how much risk you are willing to accept can help narrow down your options. For example, if you have a low risk tolerance, you may prefer funds that invest in stable, blue-chip companies or government bonds. On the other hand, if you can withstand market fluctuations for potentially higher returns, equity funds that focus on growth stocks may be appropriate.

Another critical factor is the fund's performance history. While past performance does not guarantee future results, reviewing a fund's historical returns can provide insight into how it has reacted in various market conditions. Look for funds that have demonstrated consistent performance compared to their benchmark index and peers over multiple time frames. Additionally, consider the fund's expense ratio, as lower fees can enhance your overall returns, especially in the long run.

Understanding the fund manager's investment strategy is also vital. Different managers employ various approaches to selecting securities, which can affect the fund's performance. Research the manager's track record, investment philosophy, and experience. A seasoned manager with a transparent strategy may give you confidence that your investment is in capable hands. Furthermore, ensure that the fund's strategy aligns with your financial goals and risk tolerance.

Finally, evaluate the fund’s asset allocation and diversification. A well-diversified mutual fund can help mitigate risks by spreading investments across various asset classes and sectors. Examine the fund's holdings and how they align with your investment philosophy. Ideally, you want a fund that complements your existing investments, providing a balanced approach to achieving your financial goals. By taking these steps, you can make an informed decision when selecting a mutual fund that suits your objectives and enhances your investment portfolio.

27. What are large-cap, mid-cap, and small-cap funds?

Large-cap, mid-cap, and small-cap funds are classifications of mutual funds based on the market capitalization of the companies in which they invest. Market capitalization, often referred to as market cap, is calculated by multiplying a company's current stock price by its total number of outstanding shares. This categorization is essential for investors as it helps in understanding the risk and growth potential associated with different types of companies.

Large-cap funds typically invest in companies with a market capitalization of $10 billion or more. These companies are usually well-established, have a robust financial foundation, and are leaders in their respective industries. Investing in large-cap funds is often considered less risky compared to mid-cap or small-cap funds, as these companies tend to have more stable earnings and a history of resilience during economic downturns. Retail investors looking for steady growth and lower volatility often gravitate towards large-cap funds.

Mid-cap funds focus on companies with market capitalizations between $2 billion and $10 billion. These companies are generally in a growth phase, making them more dynamic but also more volatile than their large-cap counterparts. Mid-cap funds can provide investors with an opportunity for higher returns since these companies have more room for growth and are often expanding their market share. However, this potential for growth comes with increased risk, and retail investors need to be comfortable with the possibility of greater fluctuations in their investment values.

Small-cap funds invest in companies with market capitalizations of less than $2 billion. These funds are characterized by higher volatility and risk but can also offer significant growth potential. Small-cap companies are often newer and less established, meaning they may be more susceptible to market changes and economic shifts. For retail investors willing to take on more risk in exchange for the chance of substantial returns, small-cap funds can be an attractive option. It's crucial for investors to conduct thorough research and consider their risk tolerance before investing in this category.

In summary, understanding the distinctions between large-cap, mid-cap, and small-cap funds is vital for making informed investment decisions. Each category offers varying levels of risk, growth potential, and stability. Retail investors should assess their financial goals, risk tolerance, and investment time horizon when considering these funds. By doing so, they can build a diversified portfolio that aligns with their investment objectives while navigating the complexities of the mutual fund landscape.

28. What is a fund's objective, and why is it important?

A fund's objective is the primary goal it aims to achieve through its investment strategy. This objective can vary widely among different funds, including capital appreciation, income generation, or preservation of capital. For example, a growth fund typically seeks to maximize capital gains by investing in stocks of companies expected to grow at an above-average rate, while an income fund focuses on generating regular income through dividends or interest from its investments. Understanding a fund's objective is crucial for investors, as it provides insight into the fund's investment philosophy and the types of securities it will hold.

The importance of a fund's objective lies in its alignment with an investor's personal financial goals and risk tolerance. Retail investors should carefully assess their own objectives—be they short-term gains, long-term growth, or steady income—before selecting a fund. A mismatch between an investor's goals and a fund's objective can lead to dissatisfaction and poor investment outcomes. For instance, an investor seeking steady income may be disappointed if they invest in a growth fund that prioritizes capital appreciation, which could result in higher volatility and less predictable returns.

Moreover, a fund's objective can influence its risk profile. Funds that aim for high capital appreciation often invest in more volatile assets, which can lead to significant fluctuations in value. On the other hand, funds focused on income might invest in more stable, lower-risk securities. Retail investors should carefully consider their comfort with risk and how it aligns with the fund's objective. This understanding can help prevent emotional decision-making during market downturns, as investors will have a clearer rationale for holding onto their investments.

Fund objectives are also essential for evaluating performance. Each fund is typically measured against benchmarks that reflect its stated objective. For example, a value fund might be compared to a value index, while a balanced fund could be evaluated against a blend of stock and bond indices. By understanding a fund's objective, investors can better interpret performance reports and determine whether a fund is meeting its goals relative to its peers and the market as a whole. This framework can also aid in making informed decisions about portfolio adjustments.

In summary, a fund's objective serves as a foundational element that guides its investment strategy and influences the potential risks and returns associated with it. For retail investors, aligning their investment choices with their personal financial goals is vital for successful investing. By comprehensively understanding a fund's objective, investors can make more informed decisions, reduce the likelihood of emotional reactions to market movements, and ensure that their investments are on track to meet their long-term financial aspirations.

29. How to check the track record of a mutual fund?

To check the track record of a mutual fund, investors should begin by examining its historical performance over various time frames. This includes looking at the fund's returns over one, three, five, and ten years. A longer time frame can provide a more comprehensive view of how the fund has performed through different market conditions. It is important to compare these returns against the fund's benchmark index and the performance of similar funds in the same category. This comparison helps to assess whether the fund has consistently outperformed its peers and the market.

Another critical aspect of evaluating a mutual fund's track record is understanding its volatility. A fund with high returns may seem attractive, but if it also exhibits high volatility, it may not be suitable for all investors. Metrics such as standard deviation and beta can provide insight into the fund's risk profile. A lower standard deviation indicates that the fund's returns are more stable, while a beta less than one suggests that the fund tends to be less volatile than the overall market. Understanding these metrics is essential for investors to align their risk tolerance with the mutual fund's performance history.

Investors should also consider the consistency of the fund's performance. A mutual fund that delivers strong returns in one year but underperforms in subsequent years may not be a reliable investment. Evaluating the fund manager's track record can provide insights into their investment strategy and decision-making process. Information about changes in management or significant adjustments in investment strategy can also be telling. A stable management team with a consistent investment philosophy often correlates with a more dependable fund performance.

The fund's expense ratio is another crucial factor to consider when checking its track record. High expenses can erode returns over time, making it essential for investors to factor this into their overall assessment. A lower expense ratio can enhance the net returns that investors ultimately receive. Additionally, understanding how the fund's expenses compare to other funds in the same category can provide context on whether the fees are justified based on performance.

Finally, reading through the fund's shareholder reports and fact sheets can provide valuable insights into its performance. These documents typically include detailed information about investment strategies, portfolio holdings, and performance metrics. They also often include management commentary that can shed light on the fund's future outlook. By taking the time to thoroughly review these materials, investors can make more informed decisions based on a mutual fund's track record and overall suitability for their investment goals.

30. Are past returns a reliable indicator of future performance?

When considering investments, one common belief among retail investors is that past performance can serve as a reliable indicator of future results. This notion is often expressed through the adage, "past performance is no guarantee of future results." While historical data can provide insights into how a mutual fund has performed during specific market conditions, it is essential to understand that numerous factors can influence future performance. Market dynamics, economic conditions, and changes within the fund itself can all differ from past scenarios, making it crucial for investors to approach performance data with caution.

One significant aspect to consider is the changing nature of markets. Economic cycles, interest rates, and inflation rates can shift dramatically over time, impacting the performance of mutual funds. For example, a fund that excelled during a bull market may struggle in a bear market or when economic conditions weaken. Investors must recognize that what has worked in the past may not necessarily hold true in different market environments. Therefore, while examining past returns can be informative, it should not be the sole basis for making investment decisions.

Moreover, the management of a mutual fund plays a critical role in its performance. A fund's management team may change, leading to new strategies, investment styles, or risk tolerances. These changes can significantly alter how a fund responds to market fluctuations. Investors should look beyond historical performance and consider the current management team's experience and investment philosophy. Understanding a fund's investment process, objectives, and any recent changes can provide valuable context for evaluating future performance.

Another important consideration is the impact of fees and expenses on returns. Past performance does not account for the costs associated with investing in a mutual fund, which can erode overall returns. A fund with impressive historical returns may have high management fees or other expenses that could diminish future performance. Retail investors should carefully assess a fund's expense ratio and how it might affect their investment outcomes over time. This analysis will help in making more informed decisions that account for both potential returns and costs.

Finally, while past performance can offer some insights, it should be one of many factors considered when evaluating a mutual fund. Investors should focus on a comprehensive analysis that includes current market conditions, fund management, fees, and their own investment goals and risk tolerance. By taking a holistic approach, retail investors can make more informed decisions that better align with their financial objectives, rather than relying solely on historical performance as an indicator of future success.

31. What are the risks involved in mutual funds?

Investing in mutual funds can be an effective way for retail investors to diversify their portfolios and gain exposure to various asset classes. However, like any investment, mutual funds come with inherent risks that investors should be aware of before committing their capital. Understanding these risks can help investors make informed decisions and align their investment strategies with their financial goals.

One primary risk associated with mutual funds is market risk, which refers to the possibility that the value of the fund may decline due to fluctuations in the overall market. Mutual funds typically invest in a diversified portfolio of stocks, bonds, or other securities, and the performance of these assets is influenced by economic conditions, interest rates, and investor sentiment. A downturn in the market can lead to a decrease in the value of the mutual fund, impacting the returns for investors.

Another significant risk is management risk, which arises from the decisions made by the fund's management team. Mutual funds are actively managed by professional fund managers who make investment choices on behalf of the investors. If the fund manager's strategy fails to deliver expected results or if they make poor investment choices, the fund's performance may suffer. Retail investors should evaluate the track record and investment philosophy of the fund management team to assess this risk.

Liquidity risk is also a factor to consider when investing in mutual funds. While mutual funds are generally more liquid than individual stocks, there may be instances where investors face delays in redeeming their shares, especially during periods of market volatility. Additionally, certain mutual funds, such as those investing in real estate or illiquid securities, may impose restrictions on redemptions or have longer settlement periods, which can affect an investor's ability to access their funds when needed.

Credit risk is particularly relevant for bond mutual funds, where the possibility exists that the issuers of the bonds within the fund may default on their obligations. This risk can lead to a decline in the value of the fund and reduced income for investors. Retail investors should assess the credit quality of the underlying securities in bond funds and understand how changes in interest rates can impact bond prices and overall fund performance.

Lastly, fees and expenses associated with mutual funds can also pose a risk to investors. High management fees or expense ratios can erode returns over time, particularly in cases where the fund underperforms its benchmark. Retail investors should carefully review the fee structure of any mutual fund they consider and weigh these costs against the potential benefits. By understanding and acknowledging these risks, investors can better navigate the mutual fund landscape and make choices that align with their investment objectives.

32. How do I assess my risk tolerance?

Assessing your risk tolerance is a crucial step in the investment process, especially for retail investors looking to navigate the world of mutual funds. Risk tolerance refers to the degree of variability in investment returns that an individual is willing to withstand in their investment journey. Understanding your risk tolerance helps you choose investments that align with your financial goals and comfort level, ultimately leading to a more successful investment experience.

To begin assessing your risk tolerance, it is essential to consider your financial goals. Are you investing for short-term needs, such as saving for a down payment on a house, or for long-term objectives like retirement? Short-term goals typically require a more conservative approach, as you may not have the luxury of time to recover from market fluctuations. Conversely, long-term goals allow for a higher risk tolerance since you can weather market volatility and benefit from potential growth over time.

Another factor to evaluate is your investment time horizon. The length of time you plan to keep your money invested can significantly influence your risk tolerance. A longer time horizon usually allows for more aggressive investments, as you have time to recover from potential downturns. On the other hand, if you anticipate needing access to your funds in the near future, a conservative strategy that prioritizes capital preservation may be more appropriate. This makes it vital to align your investment choices with your planned timeline for accessing your funds.

Additionally, your emotional response to market fluctuations plays a significant role in determining your risk tolerance. Some investors can handle the stress of market volatility and remain focused on long-term goals, while others may feel anxious during downturns and prefer to avoid potential losses. Reflecting on how you have reacted to past market events—such as significant drops or gains—can provide insight into your comfort level with risk. It may be helpful to discuss these feelings with a financial advisor who can guide you in determining an appropriate investment strategy.

Finally, taking a risk assessment questionnaire can provide a structured approach to evaluating your risk tolerance. Many financial institutions and investment platforms offer these questionnaires, which typically include questions about your financial situation, investment knowledge, and emotional tolerance for risk. The results can help you categorize your risk tolerance as conservative, moderate, or aggressive, guiding you in selecting mutual funds that fit your profile. By thoroughly assessing your risk tolerance, you can make informed decisions that align with your investment goals and personal comfort level.

33. Are mutual funds less risky than stocks?

Mutual funds are often perceived as a safer investment option compared to individual stocks. This perception stems from the inherent diversification that mutual funds provide. When you invest in a mutual fund, your money is pooled together with that of other investors to buy a diversified portfolio of assets. This diversification helps to mitigate risk because it reduces the impact of poor performance from any single investment within the fund. In contrast, investing in individual stocks means that the performance of your investment is directly tied to the fortunes of that particular company, which can be significantly more volatile.

The risk associated with mutual funds is also influenced by the type of fund you choose. For instance, equity mutual funds, which invest primarily in stocks, can carry a risk level similar to that of direct stock investments, especially if they focus on small-cap or growth stocks. On the other hand, bond mutual funds generally present a lower risk profile since they invest in fixed-income securities. Therefore, while mutual funds can be less risky than individual stocks in certain contexts, they are not universally lower in risk, as the specific type of mutual fund plays a crucial role in determining the overall risk exposure.

Another factor to consider is the professional management that mutual funds offer. Fund managers conduct in-depth research and analysis to select investments for the fund's portfolio, which can lead to more informed decision-making compared to individual investors who may lack the same resources or expertise. This professional oversight can help in identifying and avoiding poorly performing assets, thereby potentially reducing the risk of loss. However, it is important to note that while professional management can enhance performance, it does not eliminate risk entirely.

Investors should also be aware of the fees associated with mutual funds, which can affect overall returns. Higher fees can erode gains, especially during periods of market volatility. This factor can sometimes make mutual funds less attractive compared to individual stocks, where investors can avoid management fees altogether by purchasing shares directly. Therefore, while mutual funds may provide a risk-reduction mechanism through diversification and professional management, the costs involved must be carefully considered when evaluating their overall risk profile.

In conclusion, whether mutual funds are less risky than stocks largely depends on various factors, including the type of mutual fund, the level of professional management, and the associated fees. While mutual funds can offer a level of diversification that may reduce risk, it is essential for retail investors to perform due diligence. Understanding the specific characteristics of different mutual funds and how they align with an investor's risk tolerance and financial goals is key to making informed investment decisions.

34. What is the risk-return trade-off?

The risk-return trade-off is a fundamental concept in investing, highlighting the relationship between the potential risk associated with an investment and the expected return. In essence, this principle suggests that higher potential returns are generally associated with higher levels of risk. For retail investors, understanding this trade-off is crucial in making informed decisions about where to allocate their money, particularly in mutual funds, which vary widely in terms of risk and return profiles.

When considering investments, it is important for investors to assess their risk tolerance. Risk tolerance refers to the degree of variability in investment returns that an individual is willing to withstand. Different mutual funds cater to different risk appetites. For example, equity mutual funds tend to have higher risk due to their exposure to stock market fluctuations but offer the potential for greater returns over the long term. Conversely, bond mutual funds typically present lower risk, reflecting their steadier income streams, but they may also yield lower returns.

Investors must also take into account the time horizon for their investments. Generally, a longer investment horizon allows investors to weather market volatility, which can lead to higher returns. This is particularly relevant for mutual funds that invest in equities, as they can experience significant price fluctuations in the short term. By holding these investments over a longer period, investors can benefit from the compounding of returns and the potential recovery from market downturns.

Another critical aspect of the risk-return trade-off is diversification. By investing in a mix of different mutual funds—such as those focused on stocks, bonds, or other asset classes—investors can spread their risk. This strategy can help mitigate the potential negative impacts of any single investment's poor performance. Diversifying a portfolio allows investors to balance their risk exposure while still pursuing the desired returns, ultimately aligning their investment choices with their financial goals.

Ultimately, the risk-return trade-off is a guiding principle for retail investors navigating the world of mutual funds. By understanding the inherent risks associated with different funds and the expected returns, investors can make well-informed decisions that match their individual financial situations and investment objectives. This knowledge empowers investors to build portfolios that not only reflect their risk tolerance but also aim for growth and stability in an ever-changing market landscape.

35. How do diversification and asset allocation reduce risk?

Diversification and asset allocation are fundamental strategies in investment management that help reduce risk for retail investors. Diversification involves spreading investments across various asset classes, sectors, and geographic regions to minimize the impact of any single investment's poor performance on the overall portfolio. By holding a mix of assets, such as stocks, bonds, and real estate, investors can mitigate the volatility associated with individual investments. This approach recognizes that different assets often perform differently under varying economic conditions, and by diversifying, an investor can smooth out returns over time.

Asset allocation refers to the process of determining the optimal distribution of an investor's portfolio among different asset classes. This strategy is tailored to an investor's risk tolerance, investment goals, and time horizon. For example, a younger investor with a longer time horizon may allocate a larger portion of their portfolio to equities, which typically offer higher returns but come with greater risk. Conversely, an older investor nearing retirement may prefer a more conservative allocation, favoring fixed-income securities to preserve capital. By strategically adjusting the asset mix, investors can align their portfolios with their financial objectives and risk preferences.

Both diversification and asset allocation work together to create a balanced portfolio that can weather various market conditions. When one asset class underperforms, others may outperform, helping to cushion the impact on the overall portfolio. For instance, during a market downturn, bonds may provide stability while equities face declines. This interplay can help maintain a more consistent performance over time, reducing the likelihood of significant losses. Retail investors should understand that while these strategies do not eliminate risk entirely, they can significantly lower the potential for devastating financial impact.

Implementing diversification and asset allocation requires a thoughtful approach and regular review. Investors should periodically assess their portfolios to ensure that their asset allocation remains aligned with their goals and market conditions. Changes in personal circumstances, such as a new job or family situation, may necessitate a reevaluation of risk tolerance and investment strategy. Additionally, market fluctuations can alter the risk profile of different asset classes, making it essential to stay informed and make adjustments as needed.

In conclusion, diversification and asset allocation are key strategies for retail investors looking to manage risk effectively. By spreading investments across various asset classes and strategically determining the allocation, investors can create a portfolio that is better positioned to withstand market volatility. These practices not only help in reducing the potential for significant losses but also contribute to more stable long-term growth. Understanding and applying these concepts can empower retail investors to make informed decisions and pursue their financial goals with greater confidence.

36. Can mutual funds be used for retirement planning?

Mutual funds can play a significant role in retirement planning for retail investors. They offer a diversified investment option that can help individuals build a retirement portfolio over time. By pooling money from multiple investors, mutual funds provide access to a variety of asset classes, including stocks, bonds, and other securities. This diversification can mitigate risk and enhance the potential for higher returns, making mutual funds an attractive choice for long-term investment strategies aimed at retirement.

One of the key advantages of mutual funds in retirement planning is their flexibility. Investors can choose from a wide range of funds that align with their risk tolerance, investment goals, and time horizon. For example, equity mutual funds may appeal to younger investors with a longer time frame who can withstand market volatility, while bond funds may suit those closer to retirement seeking more stable returns. This ability to tailor investments to individual circumstances allows for a more personalized approach to retirement saving.

Moreover, mutual funds often come with professional management, which is particularly beneficial for retail investors who may lack the time or expertise to manage their investments actively. Fund managers conduct extensive research and make informed decisions on behalf of investors, adjusting portfolios as market conditions change. This professional oversight can lead to better investment outcomes and can be particularly valuable in volatile markets, where a disciplined approach to investing is crucial for preserving capital and achieving long-term goals.

Investing in mutual funds also provides the benefit of compounding returns over time. Regular contributions to a mutual fund, particularly in tax-advantaged accounts like IRAs or 401(k)s, can significantly boost retirement savings. Many mutual funds offer automatic investment plans that allow investors to contribute a set amount regularly, facilitating consistent saving habits and capitalizing on market fluctuations through dollar-cost averaging. This strategy can help investors accumulate wealth steadily as they prepare for retirement.

While mutual funds are a powerful tool for retirement planning, investors should also be aware of the associated costs, such as management fees and expense ratios, which can impact overall returns. It is essential to choose funds with fees that are reasonable and appropriate for the level of service provided. Additionally, investors should regularly review their mutual fund selections to ensure they remain aligned with their retirement goals, adjusting their strategies as necessary to adapt to changing life circumstances or market conditions. By understanding and actively managing their mutual fund investments, retail investors can effectively use these vehicles to enhance their retirement planning efforts.

37. How do I invest for short-term financial goals?

Investing for short-term financial goals requires a strategic approach that balances accessibility with potential returns. Short-term goals typically span a time frame of one to three years and may include saving for a vacation, a down payment on a house, or building an emergency fund. Given the shorter time horizon, it is crucial to prioritize investments that can provide liquidity and reduce the risk of loss, as market fluctuations can significantly impact assets held over a brief period.

One of the most suitable investment vehicles for short-term goals is money market mutual funds. These funds invest in short-term, high-quality debt instruments such as Treasury bills and commercial paper, providing a relatively stable return with low risk. Money market funds offer the advantage of liquidity, allowing investors to access their funds quickly without substantial penalties. They typically aim for a stable net asset value of one dollar per share, making them a safe choice for capital preservation while still generating some interest.

Another option for short-term investing is bond funds that focus on shorter-duration bonds. These funds invest in government and corporate bonds with maturities of one to three years. While bond funds can be subject to interest rate risk, shorter-duration bonds tend to be less volatile and can provide a reliable income stream through regular interest payments. Investors should consider the credit quality of the bonds within the fund, as higher-rated bonds generally offer lower yields but come with reduced risk.

For those who prefer a more hands-on approach, high-yield savings accounts and certificates of deposit (CDs) can also serve short-term goals effectively. High-yield savings accounts typically offer better interest rates than traditional savings accounts while maintaining easy access to funds. CDs, on the other hand, often provide higher interest rates in exchange for locking the money away for a specified term. While CDs limit liquidity, they are a low-risk option that can help investors earn more on their cash reserves without exposure to market volatility.

In conclusion, retail investors aiming to meet short-term financial goals should focus on investment options that prioritize safety and liquidity. Money market mutual funds, short-duration bond funds, high-yield savings accounts, and CDs can all play essential roles in a diversified short-term investment strategy. By carefully selecting these vehicles, investors can achieve their financial objectives while minimizing risks associated with market fluctuations.

38. Which funds are best for children's education?

When planning for children's education, selecting the right investment funds is crucial to ensure that the financial goals are met. Several types of funds can be considered, including 529 college savings plans, coverdell education savings accounts, and custodial accounts under the Uniform Transfers to Minors Act (UTMA). Each of these options offers unique benefits and tax advantages that can help maximize savings over time. Retail investors should evaluate their objectives, risk tolerance, and the time horizon until the funds will be needed.

529 college savings plans are among the most popular choices for educational savings. These plans allow contributions to grow tax-free, and withdrawals for qualified education expenses are also tax-free. Many states offer tax deductions or credits for contributions made to their own 529 plans, which can provide additional savings. Investors should consider the plan's investment options, fees, and performance history before committing to a specific 529 plan, as these factors can significantly impact overall returns.

Coverdell education savings accounts (ESAs) are another viable option for funding a child's education. ESAs also provide tax-free growth and tax-free withdrawals for qualified educational expenses, including K-12 education, which broadens their appeal. However, they have lower contribution limits compared to 529 plans and are subject to income restrictions for contributors. Retail investors should weigh the flexibility of covering both college and earlier educational expenses against the contribution limits and eligibility requirements.

Custodial accounts (UTMA) offer a different approach to saving for a child's education. These accounts allow parents to manage investments on behalf of their child until they reach the age of majority, at which point the child gains full control of the account. While UTMA accounts do not offer the same tax advantages as 529 plans or ESAs, they allow for a broader range of investment options, including individual stocks and bonds. Investors should be mindful of the potential tax implications on investment earnings, as they may be subject to the "kiddie tax" rules.

Ultimately, the best funds for children's education depend on individual circumstances, including expected education costs, investment goals, and risk tolerance. Retail investors should conduct thorough research, considering factors such as tax implications, account flexibility, and investment options. Consulting with a financial advisor may also prove beneficial, as they can provide personalized guidance and help establish a comprehensive education savings plan that aligns with the investor's overall financial strategy.

39. Can mutual funds generate a steady income?

Mutual funds can indeed generate a steady income, making them an attractive option for retail investors seeking reliable cash flow. These investment vehicles pool money from multiple investors to purchase a diversified portfolio of securities, which can include stocks, bonds, and other assets. The income generated from these investments can come in the form of dividends, interest payments, and capital gains. For those looking to receive regular income, understanding the different types of mutual funds and their income-generating potential is essential.

One popular type of mutual fund for income generation is the bond fund. These funds primarily invest in fixed-income securities, such as government and corporate bonds. Bond funds tend to pay out regular interest income, which can be distributed to investors on a monthly or quarterly basis. This makes them a suitable choice for investors who prioritize stability and predictable cash flow over high growth. However, it is important to consider the credit quality of the bonds held within the fund, as higher risk bonds may provide higher yields but also come with increased volatility and default risk.

Another option for generating income through mutual funds is through equity income funds. These funds invest predominantly in dividend-paying stocks, aiming to provide investors with a combination of capital appreciation and regular income. Companies that pay dividends are typically well-established and financially stable, which can offer a level of security for investors. Equity income funds may not provide the same level of predictability as bond funds, but they can still be a valuable source of income, particularly in a rising market where stock prices appreciate alongside dividend payouts.

Investors should also consider balanced funds, which invest in both equities and fixed-income securities. These funds aim to provide a balanced approach to income generation, combining the stability of bond investments with the growth potential of stocks. By diversifying across asset classes, balanced funds can help mitigate risk while still offering a reasonable income stream. Investors in balanced funds should pay attention to the fund's asset allocation, as it can significantly impact the income generated and the overall risk profile of the investment.

In conclusion, mutual funds can indeed serve as a reliable source of steady income for retail investors. By carefully selecting the appropriate type of mutual fund—whether it be bond funds, equity income funds, or balanced funds—investors can tailor their income strategy to meet their financial goals. It is crucial to assess each fund's objectives, risk factors, and historical performance to make informed decisions. With the right approach, mutual funds can play a key role in creating a sustainable income stream for investors seeking financial stability.

40. What is an ELSS fund, and how does it help with taxes?

An Equity Linked Savings Scheme (ELSS) is a type of mutual fund that primarily invests in equities and offers tax benefits under Section 80C of the Income Tax Act in India. ELSS funds are designed for investors looking to save on taxes while also participating in the potential growth of the stock market. The unique feature of these funds is that they have a mandatory lock-in period of three years, which means that investors cannot redeem their investments before this period expires. This lock-in period not only encourages long-term investment behavior but also aligns with the goal of wealth accumulation over time.

Investing in an ELSS fund allows retail investors to claim a deduction of up to Rs 1.5 lakh from their taxable income, thereby reducing their overall tax liability. This makes ELSS an attractive option for individuals seeking to optimize their tax planning without sacrificing the opportunity for capital appreciation. The investments made in an ELSS fund are subject to market risks, but they also have the potential for higher returns compared to traditional tax-saving instruments like Public Provident Fund (PPF) or National Savings Certificate (NSC).

The tax benefits associated with ELSS funds extend beyond the initial deduction during the investment phase. The returns generated from these funds, after the lock-in period, are treated as long-term capital gains. As of the current tax regulations, long-term capital gains exceeding Rs 1 lakh in a financial year are taxed at a rate of 10%. This tax treatment is more favorable compared to short-term capital gains, which are taxed at 15%. Therefore, ELSS funds not only help investors save on taxes upfront but can also lead to tax-efficient wealth generation over time.

Investors should consider their risk appetite and investment horizon when choosing an ELSS fund. Since these funds invest predominantly in equities, they come with a higher level of risk compared to fixed-income instruments. However, the potential for capital appreciation can be significant, especially for those who are willing to stay invested for the long term. It is advisable for investors to evaluate various ELSS funds based on their performance history, fund management, and expense ratios to make informed decisions that align with their financial goals.

In conclusion, ELSS funds serve as a strategic tool for retail investors looking to reduce their tax burden while benefiting from the growth potential of the equity markets. By combining tax savings with investment in equities, these funds cater to individuals seeking both immediate tax relief and long-term wealth creation. Investors should approach ELSS funds with a clear understanding of their financial objectives, risk tolerance, and the importance of a disciplined investment strategy to maximize the benefits of this unique financial instrument.

Section 3: Managing Your Investments (Q41–Q65)

41. What is a Systematic Investment Plan (SIP)?

A Systematic Investment Plan (SIP) is a disciplined approach to investing in mutual funds, allowing investors to contribute a fixed amount at regular intervals, typically monthly. This method is designed to facilitate systematic wealth accumulation over time, making it an attractive option for retail investors who may not have large sums to invest upfront. SIPs enable investors to take advantage of rupee cost averaging, where the cost of acquiring units is averaged out over time, reducing the impact of market volatility.

One of the primary advantages of SIPs is their affordability and flexibility. Retail investors can start with relatively small amounts, often as little as a few hundred rupees per month. This accessibility allows individuals from diverse financial backgrounds to participate in the equity markets without the burden of significant initial investments. Moreover, investors can adjust their SIP amounts and frequency as their financial situation evolves, making it a flexible investment avenue.

SIPs also encourage a long-term investment mindset. By committing to regular contributions, investors are less likely to be swayed by short-term market fluctuations or emotional decision-making. This disciplined approach fosters better investment habits and helps individuals stay focused on their financial goals. As the investment horizon extends, the compounding effect accelerates, potentially leading to substantial wealth accumulation over time.

Another critical aspect of SIPs is the ease of management. Investors can set up automatic deductions from their bank accounts, ensuring consistent contributions without manual intervention. This convenience minimizes the chances of missing out on investment opportunities due to forgetfulness or procrastination. Additionally, many mutual fund houses provide online platforms that allow investors to track their SIP performance, facilitating informed decision-making.

In conclusion, a Systematic Investment Plan offers retail investors a structured, disciplined, and flexible way to invest in mutual funds. By leveraging the benefits of rupee cost averaging, affordability, and ease of management, investors can work towards their long-term financial goals with confidence. SIPs empower individuals to enter the world of mutual fund investing, making it a practical choice for those looking to simplify their investment journey while building wealth over time.

42. How does SIP work?

Systematic Investment Plans, commonly known as SIPs, provide a streamlined method for retail investors to invest in mutual funds. SIP allows individuals to invest a fixed amount of money at regular intervals, typically monthly. This approach enables investors to build their investment portfolio over time without needing to time the market. By making smaller, consistent investments, retail investors can mitigate the risks associated with market fluctuations and benefit from the power of compounding.

The mechanics of SIP are straightforward. Investors select a mutual fund scheme and specify the amount they wish to invest regularly. The chosen amount is automatically deducted from the investor's bank account at the prescribed interval. This automated process not only simplifies the investment journey but also encourages discipline, as investors commit to investing without the temptation to time the market. Over time, the accumulation of units in the mutual fund can lead to substantial growth, depending on the fund's performance.

SIPs also leverage the concept of rupee cost averaging, which is particularly beneficial in volatile markets. When investing a fixed amount, investors buy more units when prices are low and fewer units when prices are high. This averaging effect can lead to a lower overall cost per unit over time, potentially enhancing returns. Retail investors can take advantage of market fluctuations without the stress of making investment decisions based on short-term market movements.

Another key feature of SIPs is their flexibility. Investors can start with a small amount, making it accessible to a wide range of individuals. Many mutual fund houses allow SIPs to begin with amounts as low as a few hundred rupees. Additionally, investors can increase their SIP contributions as their financial situation improves, allowing for the growth of their investments in alignment with their financial goals. This adaptability makes SIPs an attractive option for both novice and experienced investors.

In summary, SIPs offer retail investors a disciplined, effective, and flexible approach to investing in mutual funds. By committing to regular investments, leveraging rupee cost averaging, and enjoying the benefits of automation, investors can gradually build their wealth over time. SIPs not only simplify the investment process but also empower individuals to participate in the financial markets with confidence.

43. What is better: SIP or lump sum investment?

When deciding between Systematic Investment Plans (SIPs) and lump sum investments, understanding the fundamental differences is crucial for retail investors. SIP allows individuals to invest a fixed amount regularly, typically monthly, in mutual funds. This approach fosters disciplined investing and reduces the impact of market volatility by averaging the cost of investment over time. In contrast, a lump sum investment involves putting a large sum of money into a mutual fund all at once. This method can be suitable when an investor has a substantial amount of capital available and is confident in the current market conditions.

One significant advantage of SIPs is their ability to mitigate risk through rupee cost averaging. By investing consistently over time, investors buy more units when prices are low and fewer units when prices are high. This strategy can help smooth out the effects of market fluctuations, making SIPs particularly appealing for those who may not have the expertise to time the market effectively. For retail investors who prefer a hands-off approach and wish to build wealth gradually, SIPs often serve as a more prudent choice.

On the other hand, lump sum investments can be advantageous in certain scenarios, especially when the market is perceived to be favorable. If an investor has done thorough research and believes that the market is poised for growth, investing a lump sum can lead to substantial gains. This strategy can be particularly effective in a bullish market where the potential for higher returns exists. However, it also carries a higher level of risk, as market downturns can significantly impact the initial capital invested.

Investors should also consider their financial goals and risk tolerance when choosing between SIPs and lump sum investments. SIPs are generally recommended for those with a long-term investment horizon who seek to accumulate wealth without the stress of market timing. This method allows for flexibility and the ability to adjust contributions based on changing financial circumstances. In contrast, lump sum investments may suit those with a higher risk appetite who are looking for immediate exposure to the market and are prepared to withstand short-term volatility.

Ultimately, the decision between SIP and lump sum investments hinges on individual circumstances, including financial goals, market outlook, and personal risk tolerance. Retail investors should carefully assess their investment strategy and consider diversifying their approach by employing both methods at different times. By doing so, they can harness the benefits of each strategy while mitigating potential risks associated with market fluctuations. Understanding these options is key to making informed investment decisions that align with personal financial objectives.

44. How to calculate SIP returns?

To calculate the returns on a Systematic Investment Plan (SIP), investors first need to understand the concept of SIP itself. SIP is a disciplined approach to investing in mutual funds, allowing investors to contribute a fixed amount regularly, usually monthly. The returns are influenced by the market performance of the chosen mutual fund and the duration of the investment. Understanding how to calculate these returns helps investors assess their investment performance and make informed decisions.

The first step in calculating SIP returns is to determine the total investment made over the investment period. This is simply the monthly investment amount multiplied by the number of months invested. For example, if an investor contributes 5,000 each month for three years, the total investment will be 5,000 multiplied by 36 months, equaling 180,000. This figure serves as a foundation for further calculations and helps investors gauge their total commitment to the investment.

Next, investors need to calculate the future value of the SIP investments. This involves using the SIP return formula, which considers the amount invested, the expected rate of return, and the investment duration. The formula for future value (FV) of a SIP is $FV = P \times (((1 + r)^n - 1) / r) \times (1 + r)$, where P is the monthly investment amount, r is the expected monthly return rate, and n is the total number of investments. This calculation helps investors estimate how much their investments will grow over time, based on historical performance or expected market returns.

Once the future value is calculated, it is important to compare this with the total amount invested to determine the actual returns. The difference between the future value and the total investment gives the total returns earned on the SIP. This absolute return can also be expressed as a percentage by using the formula: (Total Returns / Total Investment) × 100. This percentage provides a clearer picture of how the investment performed relative to the amount put in.

Lastly, investors should consider the impact of factors like fees, taxes, and inflation on their returns. While calculating SIP returns provides a baseline understanding of performance, these additional elements can significantly affect the net gains. By accounting for these factors, investors can gain a more realistic view of their investment outcomes and adjust their strategies accordingly. Understanding how to accurately calculate SIP returns empowers investors to make better-informed choices in their mutual fund investments.

45. Can I pause or stop a SIP?

Investors often wonder about the flexibility of their investment strategies, particularly when it comes to Systematic Investment Plans (SIPs) in mutual funds. One common question is whether they can pause or stop their SIP contributions. The good news is that most mutual fund providers offer the option to pause or stop SIPs, allowing investors to manage their commitments according to their financial circumstances. This feature is particularly beneficial for those who might experience an unexpected change in income or need to redirect funds to other financial priorities.

Pausing a SIP is typically straightforward. Most mutual fund companies allow investors to temporarily halt their SIP contributions for a specified duration. This can be useful for individuals facing short-term financial challenges, such as medical emergencies or job loss, as it enables them to maintain their investment without the pressure of mandatory contributions. However, it is essential to check the specific terms and conditions with the mutual fund provider, as the duration and process for pausing a SIP can vary.

Stopping a SIP altogether is also a viable option. Investors may decide to discontinue their SIPs for various reasons, such as reaching their investment goals, changing their financial strategies, or reallocating funds to different investment avenues. When stopping a SIP, investors should be aware that this action typically involves submitting a request to their fund house. Depending on the mutual fund's policies, the request may need to be processed before the next scheduled contribution, so planning ahead is crucial.

It is important for investors to consider the implications of pausing or stopping their SIPs. While pausing can provide temporary relief, it may also disrupt the compounding effect of investments over time. Stopping a SIP could mean missing out on potential market growth and the long-term benefits of dollar-cost averaging that SIPs offer. Therefore, retail investors should carefully evaluate their financial situation and investment objectives before making a decision.

Ultimately, the ability to pause or stop a SIP provides investors with a degree of flexibility that aligns with their personal financial needs. It is advisable for investors to stay informed about the policies of their chosen mutual fund providers and to communicate with financial advisors if necessary. By understanding their options, retail investors can make informed decisions that cater to their unique circumstances while still pursuing their financial goals.

46. How often should I review my mutual fund portfolio?

The frequency with which you should review your mutual fund portfolio depends on various factors, including your investment goals, market conditions, and personal circumstances. A general guideline suggests that a comprehensive review should be conducted at least once a year. This annual assessment allows you to evaluate the performance of your funds relative to your initial investment objectives and to make informed decisions about any necessary adjustments.

In addition to the annual review, it is advisable to monitor your portfolio more regularly, such as quarterly or semi-annually. Frequent monitoring helps you stay informed about market trends and changes in the performance of your mutual funds. This doesn't mean you should react impulsively to short-term market fluctuations, but being aware of how your investments are performing can help you identify any significant deviations from your expected outcomes.

Certain life events or changes in your financial situation may also necessitate a portfolio review. Major milestones such as retirement, purchasing a home, or changes in employment can impact your investment strategy. During these times, it's crucial to reassess your risk tolerance and investment horizon to ensure your mutual fund portfolio aligns with your current financial goals and circumstances.

Market conditions can also influence how often you should review your portfolio. In periods of high volatility or economic uncertainty, more frequent reviews may be warranted. Keeping an eye on economic indicators, interest rates, and global events can provide insights into when adjustments to your portfolio may be necessary to mitigate risks or capitalize on opportunities.

Ultimately, the key is to strike a balance between staying informed and avoiding overreaction. Regular reviews should focus on assessing the alignment of your portfolio with your long-term goals rather than making hasty decisions based on short-term performance. By establishing a systematic review schedule that accounts for both personal and market factors, you can effectively manage your mutual fund investments and work towards achieving your financial objectives.

47. What should I do if my mutual fund underperforms?

If your mutual fund is underperforming, the first step is to assess the situation thoroughly. Review the fund's performance relative to its benchmark index and its peers over various timeframes. It's important to determine if the underperformance is a short-term fluctuation or part of a longer trend. Keep in mind that markets can be volatile, and mutual funds may experience periods of underperformance. Understanding the broader market context and the specific factors affecting your fund will help you make informed decisions.

Next, evaluate the fund's investment strategy and management team. Consider whether the fund's objectives align with your investment goals. If the fund's strategy has changed or it is no longer managed by a team you trust, it may be worth exploring alternatives. Look into the fund's expense ratio and fees as well; a high fee structure can eat into returns and exacerbate underperformance. Comparing these factors with other funds in the same category can provide additional insight into whether the underperforming fund is worth holding.

If you determine that the underperformance is indeed a cause for concern, consider your options. You can choose to hold the fund, believing that it may recover, or you may decide to sell it and reallocate your investments. If you opt to sell, be aware of potential tax implications, as selling may trigger capital gains taxes if the fund has appreciated in value. It's also a good idea to have a replacement investment in mind before making any moves to avoid being out of the market during a recovery phase.

Engaging with your financial advisor can provide additional clarity. They can help analyze the fund's performance and provide personalized advice based on your financial goals and risk tolerance. An advisor may also suggest diversification strategies to mitigate risks associated with underperforming funds. Regular consultations with a financial advisor can help you stay informed and make proactive adjustments to your investment strategy.

Finally, use this experience as a learning opportunity. Regularly monitoring your investments and understanding the reasons behind their performance can empower you as an investor. Make a habit of reviewing your portfolio at least annually, taking note of both the successes and failures of your investments. This proactive approach can enhance your investment knowledge and help you make better decisions in the future, ultimately guiding you toward achieving your financial objectives.

48. How to switch between mutual funds?

Switching between mutual funds can be a strategic move for retail investors seeking to optimize their investment portfolios. The process typically involves redeeming shares from one mutual fund and simultaneously investing those proceeds into another fund. This approach can help investors adapt to changing market conditions, align their investments with evolving financial goals, or take advantage of better-performing funds. However, it is essential to understand the mechanics and implications of such switches to make informed decisions.

Before initiating a switch, investors should conduct a thorough analysis of their current mutual fund holdings. This includes reviewing the fund's performance history, fees, and overall investment strategy. Additionally, investors should consider their investment objectives, risk tolerance, and time horizon. A fund that was suitable a few years ago may no longer align with the investor's current financial situation or market dynamics. By evaluating these factors, investors can determine whether a switch is warranted.

When switching funds, investors should also be aware of potential costs and tax implications. Some mutual funds charge redemption fees if shares are sold before a specified holding period, which can eat into returns. Furthermore, selling shares in a mutual fund may trigger capital gains taxes if the investment has appreciated in value. Retail investors should consult with a financial advisor or tax professional to understand these costs and ensure that the switch aligns with their overall investment strategy.

The mechanics of switching can vary depending on the mutual fund company. Some firms offer a straightforward process that allows investors to switch funds online or through customer service representatives. Others may require a more traditional approach, such as submitting a written request. It's crucial for investors to familiarize themselves with the specific procedures of their fund provider to make the transition as smooth as possible. Additionally, some mutual funds offer automatic rebalancing features that can facilitate switches without the need for direct intervention.

Finally, after completing the switch, investors should continue to monitor their new mutual fund's performance and ensure that it remains aligned with their investment strategy. Regular reviews will help investors stay on track and make further adjustments as needed. The landscape of mutual funds is continually evolving, and staying informed about new opportunities and market trends is essential for ongoing investment success. By understanding how to switch between mutual funds effectively, retail investors can enhance their portfolios and work towards achieving their financial goals.

49. Can I invest in multiple mutual funds?

Investing in multiple mutual funds is a common strategy among retail investors looking to diversify their portfolios. Diversification helps to spread risk across different asset classes and sectors, which can reduce the impact of volatility from any single investment. By investing in multiple funds, you can access a broader range of investment opportunities, potentially enhancing your returns while minimizing risk. However, it is crucial to approach this strategy with careful consideration to ensure that your investments align with your overall financial goals.

When choosing multiple mutual funds, investors should consider the types of funds they are investing in. For instance, a combination of equity funds, bond funds, and perhaps international funds can provide a balanced exposure to various markets and investment styles. It is important to evaluate how these funds interact with each other. Overlapping holdings can lead to unintended concentrations in certain sectors or asset classes, which may negate the benefits of diversification. A well-rounded portfolio typically includes funds that complement each other rather than compete for the same investment space.

Investors should also be mindful of the costs associated with investing in multiple mutual funds. Each fund may have its own management fees, expense ratios, and transaction costs. These fees can accumulate and eat into your overall returns if you are not careful. It is advisable to conduct thorough research on the cost structures of the funds you are considering and to keep an eye on how these costs will affect your investment outcomes over time. Selecting funds with competitive fees can enhance your potential for long-term growth.

Another important aspect to consider is your investment horizon and risk tolerance. Different mutual funds are designed for various investment goals, such as capital appreciation, income generation, or capital preservation. By investing in multiple funds, you can tailor your portfolio to reflect your individual risk profile and timeline. For instance, if you are a younger investor with a long time until retirement, you might choose to invest in more aggressive equity funds while balancing that with some conservative bond funds as you approach your investment goals.

In conclusion, investing in multiple mutual funds can be a strategic way to achieve diversification and manage risk. However, it requires careful planning and consideration of factors such as fund types, costs, and your personal investment objectives. By taking a thoughtful approach to your mutual fund investments, you can create a well-balanced portfolio that aligns with your financial aspirations, ultimately leading to more informed and effective investment decisions.

50. How to rebalance my mutual fund portfolio?

Rebalancing a mutual fund portfolio is a crucial strategy that helps maintain your investment goals and risk tolerance over time. As market conditions shift and certain funds perform better than others, the original asset allocation can become skewed. This drift can lead to increased risk or reduced potential returns. To rebalance effectively, start by reviewing your portfolio's current allocation compared to your target allocation, which should align with your investment objectives and risk tolerance.

The first step in the rebalancing process is to determine your target asset allocation. This allocation typically includes various asset classes such as equities, fixed income, and cash equivalents. Your target allocation should reflect your investment horizon, financial goals, and comfort with volatility. For example, a younger investor with a long time horizon may opt for a higher percentage of equities, while someone nearing retirement might prefer a more conservative approach with a larger allocation to bonds.

Once you have defined your target allocation, assess your current portfolio. Compare the actual percentages of each asset class against your target. If certain mutual funds have significantly outperformed or underperformed, you may find that your portfolio has drifted from its original allocation. For instance, if a stock fund has increased in value while a bond fund has lagged, your portfolio may now be riskier than intended. Identifying these discrepancies is essential for effective rebalancing.

The next step is to decide how to rebalance your portfolio. This can be done by either buying or selling mutual fund shares. If you need to reduce your allocation to equities, you might sell shares of your best-performing stock fund and use the proceeds to purchase shares of a bond fund or cash equivalent to bring your overall allocation back to target. Alternatively, if you prefer not to sell existing funds, you can direct new contributions to underperforming categories until your desired allocation is restored.

Lastly, consider the tax implications and transaction costs associated with rebalancing. Frequent trading can lead to capital gains taxes, which may diminish your overall returns. To minimize these effects, approach rebalancing with a long-term perspective. Many investors choose to rebalance on a set schedule, such as annually or semi-annually, or when allocations drift significantly from their targets. By regularly monitoring your portfolio and making adjustments as needed, you can maintain a balanced mutual fund portfolio that aligns with your investment strategy.

51. When should I redeem my mutual fund investments?

When considering when to redeem mutual fund investments, timing can be a critical factor in maximizing returns and minimizing losses. Investors should evaluate their financial goals, market conditions, and the specific performance of their mutual funds. Understanding these elements can help in making an informed decision about when to sell mutual fund shares.

One primary reason to redeem mutual fund investments is the achievement of financial goals. If an investor initially set a target, such as saving for a down payment on a house or funding a child's education, reaching that goal may signal the right time to liquidate part or all of the investment. Evaluating the original purpose of the investment can provide clarity on whether it has served its intended function.

Market conditions also play a significant role in the decision to redeem mutual funds. For instance, if the market is experiencing a downturn, an investor may choose to redeem their shares to prevent further losses. Conversely, during a bull market, an investor might hold off selling, anticipating that the value of their investments will continue to rise. Staying informed about economic indicators, interest rates, and overall market health can aid in determining the right moment for redemption.

Additionally, the performance of the specific mutual fund should be closely monitored. If a fund consistently underperforms compared to its benchmark or peers, it may be a sign that it is time to sell. Investors should assess the fund manager's strategy, the fund's expense ratio, and its historical performance. If there is no clear improvement or strategy to regain lost ground, redeeming the investment could be a prudent move.

Finally, personal circumstances can also influence the timing of redeeming mutual fund investments. Changes in financial situations, such as unexpected medical expenses or job loss, may necessitate accessing funds sooner than planned. It is essential for investors to remain adaptable and responsive to their financial landscape, ensuring that their investment strategy aligns with their current needs and future aspirations.

52. What is an exit load, and how does it affect withdrawals?

An exit load is a fee charged by mutual funds when an investor redeems their units before a specified period. This fee is typically a percentage of the amount withdrawn and is designed to discourage short-term trading in the fund. For example, a mutual fund may impose an exit load of 1% if units are redeemed within the first year of investment. The exit load is deducted from the redemption amount, meaning that investors receive less than the full value of their investment upon withdrawal.

The primary purpose of an exit load is to promote long-term investment in mutual funds. Mutual funds incur costs related to buying and selling securities, and frequent trading can disrupt the fund's management strategy. By imposing this fee, funds aim to stabilize their assets under management and ensure that investors remain committed for a longer duration, which can potentially lead to better returns for all investors involved.

When considering withdrawals, retail investors need to be aware of the exit load as it directly impacts the net amount they receive. If an investor decides to redeem their units shortly after purchasing them, the exit load will reduce their overall returns. This is particularly important for investors who may have invested in funds with high exit loads, as even a small percentage can significantly affect the total amount returned over time, especially on larger investments.

It is essential for investors to read the scheme information document (SID) carefully before investing in a mutual fund. This document outlines the exit load terms, including the applicable duration for which the load is charged. Understanding these details can help investors plan their investment horizon and withdrawal strategies effectively. If an investor anticipates needing access to their funds within a short timeframe, they may want to consider funds with lower or no exit loads to avoid unnecessary fees.

In summary, an exit load is a critical concept for retail investors to grasp, as it can significantly affect their investment decisions and withdrawal outcomes. By understanding how exit loads work and their implications for investment returns, investors can make more informed choices that align with their financial goals and liquidity needs. Thoughtful consideration of exit loads alongside other fund characteristics will ultimately contribute to a more strategic approach to mutual fund investing.

53. Can I partially withdraw from a mutual fund?

When considering the option to partially withdraw from a mutual fund, it's essential to understand how mutual funds work in terms of liquidity and withdrawal policies. Unlike stocks, which can be bought and sold at any time during market hours, mutual funds operate on a different principle. Investors typically buy or sell mutual fund shares at the fund's net asset value (NAV), which is calculated at the end of the trading day. This means that if you decide to make a partial withdrawal, your request will be processed at the NAV calculated after the market closes on the day your request is submitted.

Most mutual funds allow for partial withdrawals, but specific terms and conditions may vary from one fund to another. Some funds might have a minimum withdrawal amount, while others may impose restrictions on how frequently you can make withdrawals. It's important to check the fund's prospectus or consult with your financial advisor to fully understand any fees, tax implications, or penalties that may apply to partial withdrawals. Additionally, some funds may require you to maintain a minimum balance in your account after a withdrawal, which is another factor to consider.

When you make a partial withdrawal, you are essentially redeeming a portion of your investment in the mutual fund. This means that you will receive cash based on the number of shares you redeem at the current NAV. It’s crucial to note that withdrawing funds can affect your overall investment strategy and may impact your long-term financial goals. If you are withdrawing funds to meet immediate cash needs, consider how this impacts your investment's growth potential and whether it aligns with your overall financial plan.

Tax implications are also a significant factor to consider when making a partial withdrawal from a mutual fund. The portion of your withdrawal that represents capital gains may be subject to capital gains tax. If your withdrawal exceeds your original investment in the fund, you may incur additional tax liabilities. Understanding these implications can help you make informed decisions about when and how much to withdraw from your mutual fund.

In conclusion, while partial withdrawals from mutual funds are generally permitted, it is important to approach this option with careful consideration. Factors such as the fund's specific policies, potential fees, tax consequences, and the impact on your investment strategy should all be taken into account. By being informed and planning your withdrawals strategically, you can better manage your investments in a way that aligns with your financial objectives. Consulting with a financial advisor may also provide additional insights tailored to your individual circumstances.

54. What are the tax implications of redeeming mutual funds?

When redeeming mutual funds, investors need to be aware of the tax implications that can arise from the transaction. The profits generated from the sale of mutual fund shares, known as capital gains, are subject to taxation. The specific tax rate depends on how long the investor held the shares before redeeming them. If the shares were held for more than one year, the gains are typically considered long-term capital gains, which are generally taxed at a lower rate than short-term capital gains. Short-term gains, arising from shares held for one year or less, are taxed at the investor's ordinary income tax rate, which can be significantly higher.

It is also important for investors to consider whether they are redeeming shares from a taxable account or a tax-advantaged account, such as an IRA or 401(k). In a taxable account, capital gains taxes will apply upon redemption. However, if the mutual funds are held in a tax-advantaged account, investors can typically redeem shares without immediate tax consequences, deferring taxes until funds are withdrawn from the account. This distinction can have a significant impact on an investor's overall tax liability and should be taken into account when planning redemptions.

Additionally, mutual funds often distribute capital gains to their shareholders at the end of the year. These distributions may occur even if the investor has not sold any shares throughout the year. When a mutual fund realizes gains from its portfolio investments, it passes those gains on to investors, who must report them on their tax returns. This can lead to a situation where an investor may owe taxes on distributions without having sold any shares, highlighting the importance of understanding the fund's distribution policies and timing.

Investors should also be aware of the potential for tax-loss harvesting when redeeming mutual fund shares. If an investor has experienced losses in their mutual funds, they may choose to redeem those shares to realize the losses for tax purposes. These losses can offset capital gains from other investments, reducing the overall tax burden. However, it is essential to be mindful of the "wash sale" rule, which prohibits investors from claiming a tax deduction on a loss if they repurchase the same or substantially identical securities within 30 days before or after the sale.

In summary, understanding the tax implications of redeeming mutual funds is crucial for retail investors. By considering the length of time shares are held, the type of account in which the funds are held, potential capital gains distributions, and strategies like tax-loss harvesting, investors can make informed decisions that align with their overall investment goals and tax strategies. Awareness of these factors can help minimize tax liabilities and enhance the effectiveness of investment strategies in the long run.

55. How to transfer mutual funds to another person?

Transferring mutual funds to another person involves a process that requires careful consideration and adherence to specific regulations. Retail investors should first determine the type of mutual fund account they hold, as the transfer process can vary based on whether the account is held individually, jointly, or through a trust. Understanding the ownership structure is crucial, as it will dictate the necessary steps and documentation required for the transfer. In most cases, mutual funds allow for transfers to family members or other designated individuals, but each fund company may have its own policies, so it is important to consult the fund's prospectus or contact customer service for guidance.

To initiate the transfer, the investor must gather the necessary information about the mutual fund account, including the account number, the name of the fund, and the current value of the investment. The next step is to complete a transfer form, which is typically provided by the mutual fund company. This form will require details about both the transferor (the current owner) and the transferee (the new owner). It may also require signatures from both parties to authorize the transfer. Some fund companies may even require the transferee to open a new account in their name, depending on the policies in place.

Once the transfer form is completed, it should be submitted to the mutual fund company along with any additional documentation they may require. This could include identification verification for the transferee or proof of relationship between the two parties. Retail investors should be aware that the transfer process might take some time, as the mutual fund company will need to process the request and ensure compliance with all regulations. During this period, the original owner may still retain ownership rights until the transfer is officially completed.

It's also important for retail investors to consider the tax implications of transferring mutual funds. Although gifting mutual funds to another person may not trigger immediate tax liabilities, it can have consequences for both the transferor and the transferee in terms of capital gains tax upon future sales. The transferor should assess the potential impact on their tax situation, especially if the mutual funds have appreciated significantly in value. Consulting with a financial advisor or tax professional can provide clarity on how the transfer might influence taxes for both parties involved.

Lastly, retail investors should maintain clear communication with the transferee throughout the process. This ensures that both parties are aligned regarding the objectives of the transfer and any associated responsibilities. Understanding the terms of the transfer, such as whether it is a gift or a sale, can help avoid misunderstandings. Once the transfer is completed, it is advisable for the new owner to review their investment objectives and make any necessary adjustments to their portfolio based on their financial goals and risk tolerance.

56. Are mutual fund returns taxable?

Mutual fund returns can be subject to various forms of taxation, making it essential for investors to understand how these taxes may impact their overall investment returns. When you invest in mutual funds, the returns can come in different forms, including dividends, capital gains distributions, and the appreciation of the fund's net asset value. Each of these returns can have different tax implications, which can influence your investment strategy and overall financial planning.

Dividends received from mutual funds are typically taxed as ordinary income. This means that the rate at which these dividends are taxed can vary based on your income tax bracket. If the mutual fund invests in qualified dividends, they may be taxed at a lower capital gains rate, which can be significantly more favorable for investors in higher tax brackets. Understanding the nature of the dividends your mutual fund pays is crucial for anticipating your tax liability.

Capital gains distributions occur when a mutual fund sells securities within its portfolio for a profit. These gains are passed on to shareholders in the form of distributions, and they are classified as either short-term or long-term capital gains. Short-term capital gains, arising from securities held for one year or less, are taxed at the investor's ordinary income tax rate, while long-term gains benefit from a lower capital gains tax rate. This distinction is important for mutual fund investors, as it can affect the net returns on their investments.

When you eventually sell your mutual fund shares, you may also incur capital gains taxes based on the appreciation of the fund's value. The tax owed will depend on how long you held the shares before selling. If you held them for more than a year, you will be subject to long-term capital gains tax rates, which are generally more favorable than short-term rates. Conversely, if you sell shares that you held for a year or less, the gains will be taxed at your ordinary income tax rate. This makes the timing of your exit from an investment in mutual funds a critical consideration.

In addition to federal taxes, investors should also be aware of state and local taxes that may apply to mutual fund returns. Different states have varying tax laws regarding investment income, which can further impact your net returns. As such, it is advisable for investors to consider their total tax liability when evaluating mutual fund investment performance. Consulting with a tax professional can provide insights specific to your situation, helping you navigate the complexities of mutual fund taxation and optimize your investment strategy accordingly.

57. What is LTCG (Long-Term Capital Gains) tax?

Long-Term Capital Gains (LTCG) tax refers to the tax applied to profits earned from the sale of an asset that has been held for more than a year. This tax is relevant for investors who sell investments, such as stocks, bonds, or mutual funds, and realize a profit. Understanding how LTCG tax works is crucial for retail investors, as it can significantly impact the overall return on investment. The distinction between short-term and long-term capital gains is important, as short-term gains typically face higher tax rates equivalent to ordinary income tax rates.

The LTCG tax rate is generally lower than the rate applied to short-term capital gains, making long-term investments more tax-efficient. In many countries, including the United States, long-term capital gains are taxed at preferential rates, which can range from 0% to 20%, depending on the individual's income bracket. This tax structure incentivizes investors to hold their assets longer, allowing for potential growth and compounding over time while minimizing tax liabilities. For retail investors, this means that holding onto mutual funds for longer periods can enhance net returns after taxes.

Investors must also be aware of how the LTCG tax is calculated. When an asset is sold, the capital gain is determined by subtracting the purchase price, also known as the cost basis, from the selling price. Any additional costs associated with acquiring the asset, such as transaction fees, can be added to the cost basis, effectively reducing the taxable gain. It is essential for retail investors to maintain accurate records of their transactions to ensure they can correctly report their gains and minimize their tax obligations.

Another key consideration is the impact of tax-loss harvesting on LTCG tax liabilities. Investors can offset capital gains with capital losses, allowing them to reduce their overall tax burden. If an investor experiences losses in some investments, these can be used to counterbalance gains realized from other investments, potentially lowering the amount of LTCG tax owed. This strategy is particularly useful for retail investors managing a diversified portfolio, as it enhances the tax efficiency of their overall investment strategy.

Lastly, understanding the implications of LTCG tax can influence investment decisions. Retail investors should consider their investment horizon and tax situation when selecting mutual funds. Funds that focus on long-term growth may be more appealing due to the favorable tax treatment of long-term capital gains. Additionally, investors should stay informed about any changes in tax legislation that could impact LTCG rates and regulations. By incorporating LTCG considerations into their investment strategy, retail investors can optimize their tax efficiency and enhance their overall investment returns.

58. How does STCG (Short-Term Capital Gains) tax work?

Short-Term Capital Gains (STCG) tax applies to the profits made from the sale of investments held for one year or less. When retail investors buy mutual funds and sell them within this timeframe, any gain realized from the sale is considered a short-term capital gain. This applies to various types of investments, including stocks, bonds, and mutual funds. Understanding how STCG tax works is crucial for investors to effectively manage their investment returns and make informed decisions.

The tax rate for short-term capital gains is generally the same as the investor's ordinary income tax rate. This means that the income brackets and tax rates that apply to wages and salaries also apply to short-term capital gains. For retail investors, this can lead to a higher tax liability compared to long-term capital gains, which enjoy preferential tax rates. Therefore, it's essential for investors to consider the holding period of their investments when planning their investment strategies.

When investors sell mutual fund shares for a profit, they will receive a Form 1099-B from the brokerage or mutual fund company, detailing the proceeds from the sale. This form provides necessary information, including the sale date, acquisition date, and amount realized. Investors must report these gains on their tax returns, and failure to do so could result in penalties. Proper record-keeping of purchase and sale dates is crucial, as it helps in accurately determining the holding period and calculating the correct tax owed.

Investors should also be aware of the implications of STCG tax on their overall investment strategy. Frequent trading or rebalancing of a portfolio can lead to multiple short-term capital gains, potentially pushing the investor into a higher tax bracket. On the other hand, a buy-and-hold strategy can help mitigate the impact of STCG tax by allowing investments to appreciate and qualify for lower long-term capital gains rates. Therefore, investors should align their trading strategies with their tax planning to optimize their after-tax returns.

Lastly, retail investors should consider the impact of STCG tax in the context of their overall financial planning. Consulting with a financial advisor or tax professional can provide valuable insights into how to manage investments while minimizing tax liabilities. By being proactive about tax implications, investors can create a more efficient investment plan that not only focuses on growth but also on preserving wealth through effective tax management. Understanding how STCG tax works is an essential component of a comprehensive investment strategy.

59. What is a tax-saving mutual fund?

A tax-saving mutual fund, often referred to as an Equity Linked Savings Scheme (ELSS), is a type of mutual fund that offers investors the dual benefit of wealth creation and tax deductions. These funds primarily invest in equities, aiming for capital appreciation over the long term. One of the key attractions of tax-saving mutual funds is their ability to provide tax benefits under Section 80C of the Income Tax Act in many countries, allowing individuals to claim deductions on investments up to a specified limit. This makes them an appealing option for retail investors looking to reduce their taxable income while simultaneously growing their investment portfolio.

The investment in tax-saving mutual funds comes with a mandatory lock-in period of three years, which is shorter compared to other tax-saving instruments like Public Provident Fund (PPF) or National Savings Certificates (NSC). This lock-in period can be advantageous as it encourages disciplined investing and prevents premature withdrawals, allowing the invested capital to grow over time. Investors can benefit from market fluctuations, as these funds typically invest in diversified equity stocks, which can yield higher returns compared to traditional fixed-income options.

Tax-saving mutual funds also provide investors with the flexibility of systematic investment plans (SIPs), enabling them to invest small amounts regularly rather than making a lump-sum investment. This helps in averaging the cost of investment over time and reducing the impact of market volatility. Retail investors can choose to invest in these funds through SIPs, offering a more manageable approach to wealth accumulation while still enjoying the tax benefits associated with them.

In addition to tax benefits and potential for high returns, tax-saving mutual funds are managed by professional fund managers who analyze market trends and select stocks to create a balanced portfolio. This professional management is particularly beneficial for retail investors who may lack the time or expertise to manage their investments actively. By investing in tax-saving mutual funds, individuals gain access to the expertise of experienced fund managers, thereby increasing their chances of achieving their financial goals.

While tax-saving mutual funds present several advantages, it is essential for investors to consider their risk tolerance and investment horizon. Equity investments are subject to market risks, and the value of the investments may fluctuate. Therefore, it is crucial for retail investors to conduct thorough research or consult with financial advisors before investing in tax-saving mutual funds. Understanding the potential risks and rewards will help investors make informed decisions that align with their financial objectives while taking full advantage of the tax benefits these funds offer.

60. How to report mutual fund gains in tax returns?

Reporting mutual fund gains on your tax returns is a crucial aspect of managing your investments effectively. When you sell mutual fund shares for more than you paid for them, you realize a capital gain. These gains are subject to taxation and must be reported accurately on your tax return. Understanding the distinctions between short-term and long-term capital gains is essential, as they are taxed at different rates. Short-term gains, from assets held for one year or less, are taxed at your ordinary income tax rate, while long-term gains, from assets held for more than one year, benefit from lower tax rates.

To report your mutual fund gains, you will need to gather the necessary documentation. This includes your year-end statements from the mutual fund company, which will detail your transactions for the year. Specifically, you should look for the Form 1099-DIV, which reports dividends and capital gains distributions. If you sold shares during the tax year, you would also need Form 1099-B, which provides information on the sale proceeds and your cost basis. Keeping accurate records of your purchases, sales, and reinvested distributions throughout the year will make this process easier and more accurate.

Calculating your gains involves determining the difference between the selling price and your cost basis. The cost basis is generally the amount you paid for the shares, adjusted for any reinvested dividends or capital gains distributions. If you have held shares for multiple years, you may need to use specific identification methods to determine which shares you sold, particularly if you have made multiple purchases at different prices. Utilizing the average cost method can simplify this process, as it allows you to calculate an average cost basis for all your shares.

Once you have calculated your gains, you will report them on Schedule D of your tax return. This form summarizes your capital gains and losses for the year. If your gains exceed your losses, the net gain will be included in your taxable income. It's important to remember that you can also offset capital gains with capital losses, which can reduce your overall tax liability. If your losses exceed your gains, you can deduct up to $3,000 against other income, with any remaining losses carried forward to future tax years.

Lastly, keep in mind that tax laws and regulations can change, so it's wise to consult with a tax professional or financial advisor to ensure compliance and optimize your tax strategy. Utilizing tax-efficient mutual funds, such as index funds or tax-managed funds, may also help minimize tax liabilities related to capital gains. By staying informed and organized, you can effectively report your mutual fund gains and make the most of your investment returns.

61. What are mutual fund investment platforms?

Mutual fund investment platforms are online services that facilitate the buying, selling, and management of mutual fund investments. These platforms serve as intermediaries between investors and mutual fund companies, allowing retail investors to access a wide array of mutual fund options in a user-friendly environment. They offer a centralized location where investors can compare different funds, view performance histories, analyze fees, and execute transactions. This makes it easier for individuals to make informed decisions about their investments without needing extensive financial expertise.

One of the primary features of mutual fund investment platforms is their ability to provide a comprehensive overview of available mutual funds. Investors can filter funds based on various criteria, such as investment objectives, risk levels, and historical performance. Many platforms also offer tools and resources, like educational articles and market news, to help investors understand the nuances of different funds. By consolidating this information in one place, these platforms empower retail investors to conduct thorough research before committing their money.

Additionally, mutual fund investment platforms often streamline the investment process. Rather than dealing directly with multiple fund companies, investors can manage their portfolios through a single account. This not only simplifies the transaction process but also allows for easier tracking of investments. Many platforms provide features such as automatic investment plans, where investors can set up regular contributions to their chosen funds, promoting disciplined investing habits.

Fees and expenses associated with mutual fund investing can significantly impact returns, and investment platforms typically provide transparency regarding these costs. They display expense ratios, sales loads, and any other fees upfront, helping investors understand the total cost of their investments. Some platforms may also offer no-load funds, which do not charge a sales commission, making it possible for investors to keep more of their earnings. This clarity around costs is crucial for retail investors who want to maximize their investment returns.

Finally, mutual fund investment platforms often include features for monitoring and managing investment performance over time. Investors can set performance benchmarks, receive alerts on significant changes, and generate reports that summarize their investment activity. This ongoing oversight helps investors remain engaged with their portfolios and make timely decisions based on market conditions. In essence, mutual fund investment platforms not only simplify the investment process but also enhance the overall investing experience for retail investors, making it easier for them to achieve their financial goals.

62. How does FundzBazar help simplify investments?

FundzBazar serves as a comprehensive platform designed to streamline the investment process for retail investors. By providing a user-friendly interface, it simplifies the often complex world of mutual funds. Investors can easily navigate through various options, comparing different funds based on performance, risk levels, and fees. This accessibility empowers users to make informed decisions without requiring extensive financial knowledge or experience.

One of the standout features of FundzBazar is its extensive database of mutual funds. The platform aggregates information from numerous fund houses, presenting it in an organized manner. Retail investors can explore various categories such as equity, debt, and hybrid funds, allowing them to find products that align with their financial goals and risk tolerance. This centralized information hub eliminates the need for investors to scour multiple sources, saving them time and effort.

FundzBazar also offers advanced tools and resources that help investors assess their options more effectively. These tools include performance tracking, risk analysis, and historical data comparisons. Investors can visualize trends and gain insights into how different funds have performed over time. This analytical approach enables users to understand market dynamics better and make data-driven decisions, ultimately enhancing their investment strategies.

Additionally, FundzBazar emphasizes education, providing resources that cater to both novice and experienced investors. The platform features articles, tutorials, and webinars that demystify mutual fund investing. By fostering a culture of learning, FundzBazar ensures that retail investors feel more confident in their investment choices. This educational aspect is crucial, as informed investors are more likely to achieve their financial objectives.

Finally, FundzBazar simplifies the transaction process, allowing investors to purchase mutual funds directly through the platform. This direct access eliminates the need for intermediaries, reducing costs and enhancing convenience. Investors can complete transactions quickly and efficiently, managing their portfolios from one centralized location. By integrating these features, FundzBazar not only simplifies the investment process but also empowers retail investors to take charge of their financial futures.

You can use bellow links to open FundzBazar Account

For Mobile App

https://fundzbazar.com/Link/JTvifHFBFbs

For Website

https://fundzbazar.com/Link/1wPrGviIgCs

63. Are robo-advisors helpful for mutual fund investments?

Robo-advisors have emerged as a popular tool for retail investors looking to streamline their investment processes, including mutual fund investments. These digital platforms use algorithms to provide automated financial planning services with minimal human intervention. For many investors, especially those new to the investment landscape, robo-advisors can simplify the often overwhelming task of selecting mutual funds. By analyzing individual risk tolerance, investment goals, and time horizons, robo-advisors can recommend a tailored portfolio that includes a diverse range of mutual funds.

One of the primary advantages of using robo-advisors for mutual fund investments is cost-effectiveness. Traditional financial advisors often charge high fees for their services, which can eat into investment returns over time. In contrast, robo-advisors typically charge lower management fees, making them an attractive option for retail investors who are keen on maximizing their net returns. This reduction in costs is particularly beneficial for those starting with smaller investment amounts, where fees can represent a significant portion of overall returns.

Robo-advisors also employ advanced technology to ensure that investors' portfolios are well-managed over time. Many platforms offer automatic rebalancing, which helps maintain the desired asset allocation as market conditions change. This can be particularly advantageous for mutual fund investments, where maintaining a balance between equity and fixed-income funds is crucial for risk management. Additionally, robo-advisors often provide tax-loss harvesting features that can help investors minimize their tax liabilities, further enhancing overall returns.

However, while robo-advisors offer numerous benefits, they may not be suitable for every investor. The algorithm-driven approach lacks the personalized touch that a human advisor can provide, particularly for those with complex financial situations or specific investment preferences. Retail investors who value a deeper understanding of their investment choices may find the automated recommendations lacking in nuance. Furthermore, reliance on algorithms raises concerns about the adaptability of these systems to rapidly changing market conditions, which can be critical in mutual fund investing.

Ultimately, the decision to use a robo-advisor for mutual fund investments depends on individual preferences and circumstances. For retail investors seeking a straightforward, cost-effective approach to portfolio management, robo-advisors can be incredibly helpful. However, those who desire a more hands-on approach or have unique financial needs may benefit from traditional advisory services. By weighing the pros and cons of each option, investors can make informed choices that align with their financial goals and investment strategies.

64. Can I invest in mutual funds through mobile apps?

Investing in mutual funds through mobile apps has become increasingly popular among retail investors. The convenience of managing investments from a smartphone allows individuals to stay connected to their portfolios and make informed decisions on the go. Many financial institutions and asset management companies have developed user-friendly mobile applications, enabling investors to access a wide array of mutual fund options, conduct transactions, and monitor performance in real time.

To start investing in mutual funds via mobile apps, investors typically need to download the application from their preferred financial institution or mutual fund provider. After installing the app, users must create an account, which usually involves providing personal information, including identification and financial details. Most apps have robust security measures in place to protect user data, ensuring that the investment process remains secure while offering a seamless user experience.

Once an account is set up, investors can browse through various mutual fund offerings. Mobile apps often provide detailed information about each fund, including performance history, fees, and investment strategies. This accessibility allows investors to compare different mutual funds easily and make decisions based on their financial goals and risk tolerance. Additionally, many apps include educational resources and tools that help investors understand key concepts related to mutual funds, enhancing their overall investment knowledge.

Mobile apps also simplify the transaction process. Investors can purchase or redeem mutual fund shares with just a few taps on their screens. This immediacy eliminates the need for paperwork or lengthy phone calls to customer service representatives. Furthermore, many apps allow for automated investment options, such as systematic investment plans (SIPs), which enable users to invest a fixed amount regularly. This feature can help retail investors maintain discipline in their investment strategies.

While mobile apps offer significant advantages, it is crucial for investors to remain vigilant about potential risks. Market volatility can quickly affect mutual fund values, and the ease of trading may lead some investors to make impulsive decisions. Therefore, it's essential to have a well-thought-out investment strategy and to review personal financial goals regularly. By leveraging the benefits of mobile apps while practicing sound investment principles, retail investors can effectively manage their mutual fund investments.

65. How to compare mutual funds online?

Comparing mutual funds online is an essential step for retail investors seeking to make informed investment decisions. The internet offers a wealth of resources that allow investors to evaluate various mutual funds based on several criteria. One of the primary factors to consider is the fund's performance history. Investors should look at the fund's returns over different time frames, such as one year, five years, and ten years, to gauge its consistency and reliability. Online fund comparison tools often provide this information, allowing investors to see how a fund has performed relative to its benchmark index and other funds within the same category.

Another crucial aspect to consider when comparing mutual funds is the expense ratio. This figure represents the annual fee that all mutual funds charge their shareholders, expressed as a percentage of the fund's assets. A lower expense ratio can significantly impact an investor's overall returns, especially over the long term. Retail investors can find detailed expense ratio information on financial websites that aggregate data on various funds, making it easier to identify funds that align with their cost preferences. Additionally, understanding what is included in these fees, such as management fees and administrative costs, is vital for making a comprehensive comparison.

Investors should also pay close attention to the fund's investment strategy and objectives. Not all mutual funds are created equal; some are designed for aggressive growth, while others aim for stability and income generation. By reading the fund's prospectus, which is often available online, investors can gain insights into the underlying assets, geographic focus, and investment philosophy of the fund. Understanding these elements helps retail investors ensure that their chosen mutual funds align with their risk tolerance and investment goals.

Another effective way to compare mutual funds is to look at qualitative factors, such as the fund manager's experience and the management team's track record. Many financial news websites and investment research platforms provide profiles and interviews with fund managers, which can offer valuable insights into their investment strategies and decision-making processes. A seasoned manager with a successful history can be a significant indicator of a fund's potential for future success. Retail investors should also consider the stability of the management team, as frequent turnover can impact a fund's performance.

Lastly, utilizing online forums and investor communities can provide additional perspectives when comparing mutual funds. These platforms allow investors to share experiences, insights, and performance reviews of specific funds. Engaging with other retail investors can help individuals uncover potential red flags or hidden gems that may not be immediately apparent through traditional comparison tools. By combining quantitative metrics with qualitative insights and community feedback, retail investors can make more informed decisions when selecting mutual funds that best suit their financial objectives.

Section 4: Advanced Topics and Myths (Q66–Q95)

66. What is a fund benchmark?

A fund benchmark is a standard or point of reference against which the performance of a mutual fund can be measured. It serves as a comparative tool that helps investors understand how well a fund is performing relative to a specific segment of the market or to a particular investment strategy. Typically, benchmarks are constructed from a selection of securities that represent an index or a group of assets, and they are crucial in evaluating the effectiveness of fund management.

Most mutual funds will be compared to a relevant benchmark index that represents the type of securities in which the fund invests. For example, a large-cap equity fund might use the S&P 500 index as its benchmark, while a bond fund might compare its performance to the Bloomberg Barclays U.S. Aggregate Bond Index. These benchmarks are chosen based on the fund's investment objective and strategy, providing a relevant context for performance evaluation.

Investors use benchmarks to assess whether a fund manager is delivering adequate returns relative to the risk taken. A fund that consistently outperforms its benchmark may be seen as a sign of effective management and investment skill. Conversely, underperformance against the benchmark could raise concerns regarding the fund's management, prompting investors to reevaluate their investment choices. This performance comparison helps in making informed decisions about whether to buy, hold, or sell fund shares.

It is important to note that while benchmarks are useful for performance evaluation, they do not account for all aspects of fund performance. Factors such as risk-adjusted returns, fees, and market conditions also play significant roles in a fund's overall performance. Therefore, investors should consider these elements alongside benchmark comparisons when assessing a mutual fund's viability as part of their investment portfolio.

In summary, fund benchmarks are critical tools for retail investors looking to evaluate mutual fund performance. They provide a clear and quantifiable way to measure how well a fund is doing relative to a defined market segment. By understanding the role of benchmarks, investors can make more informed decisions, assess the effectiveness of fund management, and ultimately enhance their investment strategies.

67. How to interpret fund fact sheets?

Understanding fund fact sheets is essential for retail investors seeking to make informed decisions about mutual funds. A fund fact sheet serves as a concise summary of a mutual fund's key information, typically encompassing performance metrics, investment objectives, and management insights. By familiarizing yourself with the essential components of a fund fact sheet, you can effectively assess whether a particular fund aligns with your investment goals and risk tolerance.

The first aspect to examine in a fund fact sheet is the fund's investment objective. This section outlines the primary aim of the fund, such as capital appreciation, income generation, or a combination of both. Understanding the investment objective helps you determine whether the fund's strategy aligns with your financial goals. For instance, if you are seeking long-term growth, a fund focused on equity investments may be more suitable than one prioritizing fixed income.

Next, pay close attention to the performance data provided in the fact sheet. This typically includes historical returns over various time frames, such as one, three, and five years. While past performance is not a guarantee of future results, it can give you insight into how the fund has reacted to different market conditions. Additionally, comparing the fund's performance against a relevant benchmark index can help you evaluate its effectiveness. A fund that consistently outperforms its benchmark may indicate strong management and a sound investment strategy.

Another critical component is the expense ratio, which reflects the costs associated with managing the fund. A lower expense ratio can significantly impact your overall investment returns over time. Retail investors should compare the expense ratios of similar funds to ensure they are not overpaying for management. Additionally, understanding any sales charges or fees associated with buying or redeeming shares is equally important, as these can further affect your net returns.

Finally, consider the fund manager's experience and the fund's management style, which are often detailed in the fund fact sheet. A seasoned manager with a successful track record may inspire confidence, while a newer manager may require more scrutiny. The management style, whether active or passive, can also influence performance and risk levels. By combining insights from the investment objective, performance data, expenses, and management details, retail investors can make more informed investment decisions and select mutual funds that best suit their individual financial needs.

68. What is the Sharpe ratio?

The Sharpe ratio is a key metric used by investors to evaluate the performance of an investment compared to its risk. Developed by William F. Sharpe, this ratio measures the excess return that an investor receives for taking on additional risk. In simpler terms, the Sharpe ratio quantifies how much return an investor is earning for each unit of risk they are assuming. This is particularly useful in the context of mutual funds, where investors are often faced with a variety of options that carry different risk levels.

To calculate the Sharpe ratio, an investor takes the return of the investment, subtracts the risk-free rate (often represented by the yield on government bonds), and divides this result by the standard deviation of the investment's returns. The formula looks like this: Sharpe Ratio = (Return of the Portfolio - Risk-Free Rate) / Standard Deviation of the Portfolio's Returns. A higher Sharpe ratio indicates a more attractive risk-adjusted return, signaling that the investment may deliver better returns for the amount of risk taken.

For retail investors, understanding the Sharpe ratio can be particularly beneficial when comparing different mutual funds. Two funds may have similar nominal returns, but their risk profiles could be vastly different. By looking at the Sharpe ratios, investors can gain insight into which fund is providing a better return relative to the risk involved. This can help investors make more informed decisions, aligning their choices with their own risk tolerance and investment goals.

It is important to note that while the Sharpe ratio is a valuable tool, it is not without its limitations. For instance, the ratio assumes that returns are normally distributed, which may not always be the case in real-world scenarios. Additionally, the Sharpe ratio can be affected by the time period over which it is calculated, as market conditions can change dramatically. Therefore, investors should consider using the Sharpe ratio alongside other performance metrics to get a comprehensive view of a mutual fund's potential.

In conclusion, the Sharpe ratio serves as a crucial measure for retail investors seeking to understand the relationship between risk and return in mutual funds. By focusing on the risk-adjusted return, investors can make more strategic choices that align with their financial objectives. As they navigate the complexities of mutual fund investing, incorporating the Sharpe ratio into their analysis can enhance their ability to identify funds that not only perform well but do so while managing risk effectively.

69. What is alpha and beta in mutual fund analysis?

Alpha and beta are two critical metrics used to evaluate the performance of mutual funds, helping investors understand risk and return dynamics. Alpha measures a fund's performance relative to a benchmark index, reflecting the value added by the fund manager's investment decisions. A positive alpha indicates that the fund has outperformed its benchmark, while a negative alpha suggests underperformance. For retail investors, understanding alpha is crucial because it provides insight into how well a fund manager is navigating market conditions to generate excess returns.

Beta, on the other hand, measures a fund's volatility in relation to the overall market. A beta of 1 indicates that the fund's price movements are closely aligned with the market. A beta greater than 1 suggests that the fund is more volatile than the market, meaning it could experience larger price swings during market fluctuations. Conversely, a beta less than 1 indicates lower volatility compared to the market. For retail investors, knowing a fund's beta helps assess the risk associated with investing in that fund, guiding them in aligning their investment choices with their risk tolerance.

When analyzing mutual funds, it is essential to consider both alpha and beta together. While alpha provides insight into a fund's ability to generate excess returns, beta offers a view of the associated risks. For instance, a fund with a high alpha but also a high beta may be appealing for investors seeking high returns, but it may also involve significant risk. Conversely, a fund with a low beta may be more suitable for risk-averse investors, even if it has a lower alpha. This dual perspective allows investors to make more informed decisions based on their investment goals and risk appetite.

Investors should also be aware of the limitations of alpha and beta. These metrics are based on historical performance and may not accurately predict future results. Factors like changes in market conditions, economic events, or shifts in management strategy can impact both alpha and beta over time. Therefore, while these metrics are valuable tools for analysis, they should not be the sole criteria for selecting a mutual fund. Investors should consider a comprehensive set of factors, including fund objectives, fees, and the manager's investment philosophy.

In summary, understanding alpha and beta is essential for retail investors looking to evaluate mutual funds effectively. Alpha serves as a measure of a fund manager's skill in achieving returns beyond a benchmark, while beta indicates the fund's risk profile relative to market fluctuations. By interpreting these metrics together, investors can gain a deeper insight into potential rewards and risks, enabling them to align their investment strategies with their financial goals. However, it is crucial to supplement this analysis with a broader assessment of the fund's overall characteristics to ensure a well-rounded investment approach.

70. How do index funds differ from actively managed funds?

Index funds and actively managed funds represent two distinct approaches to investing in the stock market. Index funds are designed to replicate the performance of a specific market index, such as the S&P 500, by holding the same securities in the same proportions as the index. This passive investment strategy aims to achieve market returns rather than outperform them. On the other hand, actively managed funds involve a team of portfolio managers who make decisions about which securities to buy and sell based on research, market conditions, and their investment philosophies. This active approach seeks to generate higher returns than the market average by identifying undervalued stocks or market trends.

One of the primary differences between index funds and actively managed funds is their cost structure. Index funds typically have lower expense ratios because they do not require the same level of management and research as actively managed funds. The passive nature of index funds means they can be managed with fewer resources, allowing for reduced fees. Conversely, actively managed funds usually come with higher fees to compensate portfolio managers for their expertise and the extensive research efforts that inform their investment choices. For retail investors, this difference in costs can significantly impact long-term investment returns, as higher fees tend to erode gains over time.

Performance is another key area where index funds and actively managed funds differ. Historically, many actively managed funds have struggled to consistently outperform their benchmark indexes, particularly after accounting for fees. While some managers may achieve short-term success, studies have shown that the majority of actively managed funds fail to beat their respective indexes over the long term. In contrast, index funds, by design, match the market returns, which can be appealing to investors seeking a straightforward investment strategy that minimizes the risk of underperformance.

Tax efficiency is also a crucial consideration when comparing these two types of funds. Index funds tend to be more tax-efficient because they have lower turnover rates, meaning they buy and hold securities for longer periods. This strategy results in fewer taxable events, such as capital gains distributions, which can benefit investors in taxable accounts. Actively managed funds, however, often engage in frequent trading to capitalize on market opportunities, leading to higher turnover and potentially more significant tax liabilities for investors. Retail investors should consider the tax implications of each fund type based on their individual financial situations.

Ultimately, the choice between index funds and actively managed funds depends on an investor's goals, risk tolerance, and investment philosophy. Index funds may be more suitable for those who prefer a hands-off approach and seek to achieve market returns at a lower cost. In contrast, investors who believe in the potential for skilled management to outperform the market may lean towards actively managed funds. Understanding these differences is essential for retail investors as they navigate the complex landscape of mutual fund investing and strive to build a diversified portfolio that aligns with their financial objectives.

71. Are mutual funds only for wealthy investors?

Mutual funds are often perceived as investment vehicles primarily accessible to wealthy individuals, but this view is misleading. In reality, mutual funds are designed to cater to a wide range of investors, including those who are just starting to build their portfolios. The structure of mutual funds allows individuals to invest with relatively small amounts, making them an attractive option for retail investors. With minimum investment amounts that can be as low as a few hundred dollars, mutual funds provide an entry point for anyone looking to invest, irrespective of their wealth status.

One of the key advantages of mutual funds is the professional management they offer. Fund managers, who are typically well-versed in market trends and investment strategies, handle the selection and management of the fund's assets. This means that individual investors do not need to have extensive knowledge or experience in investing to participate. The pooling of funds from many investors allows for diversification, which is beneficial for managing risk. Therefore, even retail investors with limited capital can enjoy the benefits of a well-managed investment portfolio.

Moreover, mutual funds come in various types, catering to different risk appetites and investment goals. For instance, there are equity funds, bond funds, balanced funds, and index funds, each with unique characteristics and potential returns. This diversity means that investors can choose funds that align with their financial objectives, whether they are looking for growth, income, or capital preservation. Retail investors can create a balanced portfolio by selecting a mix of mutual funds, thereby enhancing their chances of achieving their investment goals over time.

The accessibility of mutual funds is further enhanced by the rise of technology and online investment platforms. Many financial institutions and brokerage firms now offer easy access to mutual funds through their websites and mobile applications. This allows retail investors to research, compare, and invest in mutual funds with just a few clicks. Additionally, some platforms have eliminated investment minimums or offered no-load funds, further democratizing access to these investment vehicles and allowing even those with modest incomes to invest.

In conclusion, mutual funds are not exclusively for wealthy investors. They are accessible, versatile, and designed to meet the needs of various investors, including retail individuals. With a variety of options available and the ability to start investing with relatively low amounts, mutual funds provide a practical way for anyone to participate in the financial markets. As a result, they serve as an effective tool for building wealth over time, regardless of an investor's starting financial position.

72. Do mutual funds guarantee returns?

Mutual funds do not guarantee returns, and understanding this is crucial for retail investors. Unlike fixed-income investments such as bonds or bank deposits, mutual funds are subject to market risks and fluctuations. The performance of a mutual fund is influenced by various factors, including the economic environment, interest rates, and the performance of the underlying securities within the fund. As a result, the value of mutual fund shares can go up or down, and past performance is not indicative of future results.

Investors often seek the safety of guaranteed returns, which can lead to misconceptions about mutual funds. It is essential to recognize that while mutual funds may aim to provide growth or income, they inherently carry risks. For example, equity mutual funds invest primarily in stocks, which can be volatile and subject to market swings. Conversely, bond funds may provide more stability, but they also carry risks related to interest rate changes and credit quality. Therefore, investors should assess their risk tolerance and investment goals when considering mutual funds.

Some mutual funds offer features that can provide a semblance of stability, such as target-date funds or those with a focus on income generation. However, these funds still do not guarantee returns. Target-date funds adjust their asset allocation over time, becoming more conservative as the target date approaches, yet they remain exposed to market risks. Income-focused funds may provide regular distributions, but the underlying assets can still fluctuate in value, impacting overall returns.

Investors should also be aware of the fee structure associated with mutual funds. High management fees can erode returns over time, making it even more challenging to achieve positive performance. Retail investors must carefully evaluate mutual fund expenses and select funds that align with their investment strategy to maximize their potential returns. Understanding the impact of fees is crucial to achieving favorable investment outcomes.

In conclusion, while mutual funds offer a diversified investment option and the potential for growth, they do not guarantee returns. Retail investors must approach mutual funds with a clear understanding of the risks involved and set realistic expectations based on market conditions. By focusing on long-term investment goals and maintaining awareness of the inherent risks, investors can make informed decisions that align with their financial objectives.

73. Is it better to invest only during market lows?

Investing during market lows can seem appealing due to the potential for purchasing assets at discounted prices. However, it is essential to understand that timing the market is notoriously difficult. Many investors believe that by only investing during downturns, they can maximize their returns. While this strategy can yield significant profits if executed correctly, it also carries considerable risk and may not be the most prudent approach for the average retail investor.

One of the main issues with investing solely during market lows is the unpredictability of market movements. Markets can remain low for extended periods, or they may rebound unexpectedly. If an investor waits for the perfect moment to enter the market, they might miss out on substantial gains during recoveries. This phenomenon, known as "missing the market," illustrates how even brief periods of market upswings can substantially impact overall investment performance. For retail investors, regularly contributing to investments, regardless of market conditions, tends to yield better long-term results.

Another factor to consider is the emotional aspect of investing. Investors often experience fear and anxiety during market downturns, which can lead to impulsive decisions. By committing to a strategy of only investing at market lows, investors may find themselves paralyzed by uncertainty or may fail to act when opportunities arise. A more consistent approach to investing, such as dollar-cost averaging, can help mitigate emotional decision-making by spreading out investments over time. This strategy allows investors to buy more shares when prices are low and fewer when prices are high, ultimately balancing the cost per share.

The benefits of diversification also come into play when considering the timing of investments. By investing consistently, retail investors can build a diversified portfolio that includes various asset classes, thereby reducing risk. Concentrating investments solely during market lows can lead to a lack of diversification, making portfolios more vulnerable to market fluctuations. A well-rounded approach that incorporates regular investments across different market conditions can help achieve a more stable and resilient investment strategy.

In conclusion, while investing during market lows can provide opportunities for significant gains, it is not the only strategy that retail investors should consider. The unpredictability of markets, emotional factors, and the importance of diversification suggest that a more consistent and disciplined investment approach may be more beneficial over the long term. Retail investors are encouraged to adopt a strategy that aligns with their financial goals and risk tolerance, allowing for steady growth regardless of market conditions.

74. Are mutual funds risk-free?

Mutual funds are often perceived as a safer investment vehicle compared to individual stocks, primarily because they offer diversification. By pooling money from multiple investors, mutual funds can invest in a broad array of assets, including stocks, bonds, and other securities. This diversification helps to spread risk, as the poor performance of one investment can be offset by better performance in others. However, this does not mean that mutual funds are risk-free. Investors should understand the various types of risks associated with mutual funds before considering them as a guaranteed safe investment option.

One of the primary risks associated with mutual funds is market risk, which refers to the potential for losses due to fluctuations in the market. Even diversified portfolios can experience declines in value, particularly during economic downturns. For instance, equity mutual funds may see their values drop significantly if the stock market faces a bear phase. Similarly, bond mutual funds may be affected by changes in interest rates, which can lead to decreased bond prices. Consequently, while mutual funds can mitigate some risks through diversification, they are still subject to the inherent volatility of the markets.

Another risk to consider is management risk, which arises from the decisions made by the fund managers. Each mutual fund is managed by professionals who make investment choices based on their strategies and outlook on the market. If a fund manager makes poor investment decisions or fails to react appropriately to market changes, it can result in underperformance of the fund. This risk underscores the importance of researching fund managers and their historical performance before investing in a mutual fund.

Additionally, investors should be aware of liquidity risk, which pertains to the ease with which assets can be bought or sold without significantly affecting their price. While most mutual funds are relatively liquid, meaning investors can buy or sell shares at the end of each trading day, some funds may invest in assets that are not easily tradable. In times of financial crisis, these illiquid assets can lead to difficulties in selling shares at favorable prices. Understanding the liquidity profile of a mutual fund is essential for investors who may need to access their funds quickly.

Lastly, it is crucial to consider that mutual funds come with fees and expenses that can impact overall returns.

Management fees, sales loads, and other expenses can erode investment gains over time. Higher fees do not always correlate with better performance, so investors should carefully assess the cost structures of mutual funds before investing. While mutual funds can be a valuable component of a diversified investment strategy, they are not risk-free. By understanding the various risks and costs involved, retail investors can make more informed decisions and better navigate the complexities of mutual fund investing.

75. Can mutual funds make you rich quickly?

Mutual funds are often marketed as a viable investment option for individuals looking to grow their wealth over time. However, the idea that they can make you rich quickly is a misconception that needs to be addressed. While mutual funds can provide a means for wealth accumulation, they typically require a longer investment horizon to realize significant gains. The performance of mutual funds is influenced by various factors, including market conditions, fund management, and the underlying assets in which they invest. As such, expecting rapid wealth accumulation from mutual funds can lead to disappointment.

One of the primary advantages of mutual funds is diversification. By pooling money from multiple investors, mutual funds can invest in a broad range of securities, which helps mitigate risks associated with investing in individual stocks or bonds. This diversification can lead to more stable returns over time. However, the trade-off is that while mutual funds can deliver substantial returns, they are not designed for quick wealth generation. The market fluctuations that may provide short-term gains can just as easily lead to losses, underscoring the importance of a long-term investment strategy.

Another critical aspect to consider is the impact of fees and expenses on mutual fund performance. Management fees, administrative costs, and sales charges can erode returns, particularly in funds that do not outperform the market. Retail investors should carefully evaluate the expense ratios of mutual funds before investing, as these costs can significantly affect overall returns. A fund that seems to have performed well historically may not necessarily continue to do so, especially after accounting for fees. Therefore, it is essential to focus on funds with a solid track record of performance relative to their costs.

Moreover, market timing is often touted as a strategy for quick wealth accumulation, but it is notoriously difficult to execute successfully. Many investors attempt to buy mutual funds when they believe prices are low and sell when they are high, yet this approach can lead to poor decision-making. Instead of trying to time the market, a more effective strategy is dollar-cost averaging, where investors regularly contribute to their mutual fund investments regardless of market conditions. This method can help smooth out the effects of market volatility over time and contribute to wealth accumulation.

Ultimately, while mutual funds can be a valuable component of an investment portfolio, they should not be viewed as a shortcut to instant riches. Retail investors should approach mutual fund investing with realistic expectations, focusing on long-term growth potential rather than quick gains. By understanding the fundamentals of mutual funds, including diversification, fees, and the importance of a disciplined investment strategy, investors can better position themselves for financial success over time.

76. Can mutual funds invest in gold?

Mutual funds can indeed invest in gold, but the manner and extent of such investments can vary widely among different types of funds. Some mutual funds directly invest in physical gold, while others may invest in gold-related assets, such as stocks of mining companies or exchange-traded funds (ETFs) that track the price of gold. Understanding these options is crucial for retail investors who want to diversify their portfolios with gold exposure.

Funds that invest directly in physical gold are typically classified as specialized or commodity-focused funds. These funds purchase gold bullion or coins and hold them in secure storage. This approach allows investors to gain direct exposure to gold prices, which can serve as a hedge against inflation or economic downturns. However, investing in physical gold through mutual funds comes with specific considerations, such as storage costs and insurance that can impact overall returns.

On the other hand, many mutual funds choose to invest in gold indirectly through equities. These funds may hold shares of gold mining companies, which can offer leveraged exposure to gold prices. When gold prices rise, mining companies often see a significant increase in profitability, resulting in potentially higher returns for investors. However, this strategy also carries risks, as mining operations are susceptible to operational challenges, regulatory changes, and fluctuations in production costs, which can all affect stock performance.

Additionally, there are mutual funds that incorporate gold ETFs into their portfolios. These funds invest in ETFs that track the price of gold, allowing investors to gain exposure without the complexities of holding physical gold. This method offers liquidity and ease of trading, as ETFs can be bought and sold like regular stocks on exchanges. Retail investors should evaluate the management fees and expense ratios associated with these funds, as they can impact long-term investment performance.

In summary, mutual funds can invest in gold through various channels, including direct ownership of physical gold, shares of mining companies, or gold-related ETFs. Each method carries its own set of advantages and risks, which retail investors should carefully consider in the context of their investment goals and risk tolerance. By understanding these options, investors can make informed decisions about how to incorporate gold into their portfolios.

77. What are exchange-traded funds (ETFs)?

Exchange-traded funds (ETFs) are investment funds that are traded on stock exchanges, similar to individual stocks. They hold a collection of assets, such as stocks, bonds, or commodities, and their value fluctuates throughout the trading day based on market demand. ETFs are designed to track the performance of a specific index, sector, or asset class, providing investors with exposure to a diversified portfolio without having to buy each individual security. This makes them an appealing option for retail investors looking to simplify their investment strategies.

One of the key characteristics of ETFs is their structure. Unlike mutual funds, which are generally bought and sold at the end of the trading day at the net asset value (NAV), ETFs can be bought and sold at any time during market hours at market prices. This feature allows investors to take advantage of price fluctuations throughout the day and to implement various trading strategies, such as short selling and options trading. The ability to trade ETFs like stocks adds a level of flexibility and liquidity that many investors find attractive.

ETFs also offer a cost-effective way to invest. They typically have lower expense ratios than mutual funds due to their passive management style, which aims to replicate the performance of an index rather than actively selecting securities. Additionally, because ETFs are traded on an exchange, investors may incur lower transaction costs compared to mutual funds, which often require minimum investment amounts and may charge sales loads. As a result, retail investors can gain exposure to a wide array of assets with relatively low fees, enhancing their overall investment returns.

Tax efficiency is another advantage of ETFs that appeals to retail investors. When investors sell shares of a mutual fund, capital gains taxes may be triggered for all shareholders, regardless of whether they sold their shares. In contrast, ETFs typically allow investors to manage their tax liabilities more effectively due to their unique structure. The "in-kind" creation and redemption process helps minimize taxable events, making ETFs a more tax-efficient investment vehicle. This can lead to improved after-tax returns, particularly for investors in higher tax brackets.

While ETFs offer numerous benefits, there are also considerations to keep in mind. Investors should be aware of the potential for trading costs, such as commissions and bid-ask spreads, which can impact overall returns. Additionally, the wide variety of ETFs available means that investors must conduct thorough research to select the right options that align with their investment goals and risk tolerance. Overall, understanding the fundamentals of ETFs equips retail investors with the tools needed to make informed decisions in their investment journey.

78. What is a dividend payout option in mutual funds?

A dividend payout option in mutual funds refers to a specific choice investors have regarding how they receive income generated by the fund's investments. When a mutual fund earns income from dividends, interest, or capital gains, it can distribute this income to its shareholders. The dividend payout option allows investors to receive these distributions in cash, which can be particularly appealing for those who rely on this income for regular expenses or to supplement their earnings.

Investors can choose between different options when they invest in mutual funds. The dividend payout option is one of several choices available, including the reinvestment option, where dividends are automatically reinvested into additional shares of the fund. This option is essential for investors who prefer immediate cash flow rather than growing their investment through reinvestment. Understanding these choices can help investors align their portfolio strategies with their financial goals and cash flow needs.

The frequency of dividend payouts can vary depending on the mutual fund's policy and the type of income generated. Some funds may distribute dividends quarterly, while others do so annually or semi-annually. Investors should pay attention to these schedules, as they can impact cash flow management. Additionally, the amount of the dividend payout can fluctuate based on the fund's performance and the overall market conditions, making it crucial for investors to stay informed about their chosen fund's performance.

It's important to note that a dividend payout does not guarantee a profit for the investor, as it is subject to the fund's overall performance. Funds that offer higher dividend payouts may not always be the best option, as they could indicate higher risk or less potential for capital appreciation. Retail investors should carefully evaluate the fund's investment strategy, past performance, and the sustainability of its dividend payments before making a decision.

In summary, the dividend payout option in mutual funds provides investors with an opportunity to receive income from their investments in cash rather than reinvested shares. This option is particularly beneficial for those seeking regular income but requires careful consideration of various factors, including the fund's distribution frequency and sustainability. By understanding the implications of choosing a dividend payout option, retail investors can make informed decisions that align with their financial objectives and risk tolerance.

79. Can mutual funds invest in real estate?

Mutual funds typically do not invest directly in physical real estate properties. Instead, they may invest in real estate-related securities, such as real estate investment trusts (REITs), which are companies that own, operate, or finance income-producing real estate. By including REITs in their portfolios, mutual funds can provide investors with exposure to the real estate market without the complexities of owning physical properties. This allows investors to benefit from the potential appreciation in property values and income generated from rental payments while maintaining the liquidity of their investment.

Investing in mutual funds that focus on real estate can be an effective way for retail investors to diversify their portfolios. Real estate often behaves differently from stocks and bonds, which means that it can help reduce overall portfolio risk when included as part of a broader investment strategy. By allocating a portion of their investments to real estate-focused mutual funds, investors can potentially enhance returns while mitigating volatility, as real estate markets may not always move in tandem with equity or fixed-income markets.

Some mutual funds specifically target the real estate sector, investing primarily in REITs and other real estate-related securities. These funds may focus on different types of real estate, such as residential, commercial, or industrial properties, each with its own risk and return profile. Retail investors should be aware of the specific focus of a mutual fund when considering an investment, as the performance of these funds can be influenced by factors such as interest rates, economic conditions, and regional real estate trends.

When evaluating mutual funds that invest in real estate, it is crucial for investors to consider the fund's expense ratio, historical performance, and the expertise of the fund manager. High fees can erode investment returns over time, so finding a fund with a reasonable expense ratio is essential. Additionally, reviewing the fund's past performance in various market conditions can provide insights into how well the fund is managed and its responsiveness to changes in the real estate market.

In summary, while mutual funds do not typically invest directly in physical real estate, they can provide retail investors with access to the real estate market through investments in REITs and other real estate-related securities. This approach allows investors to diversify their portfolios and potentially reap the benefits of real estate investments without the challenges of direct property ownership. As with any investment, understanding the specific characteristics and risks of real estate-focused mutual funds is key to making informed investment decisions.

80. What are liquid funds?

Liquid funds are a category of mutual funds that primarily invest in short-term debt instruments and money market securities. These funds are designed to provide investors with high liquidity, low risk, and a reasonable return on investment. Liquid funds typically invest in securities with maturities of up to 91 days, such as treasury bills, commercial papers, certificates of deposit, and other similar short-term instruments. This short maturity profile helps in minimizing interest rate risk, making liquid funds an attractive option for retail investors seeking a safe parking place for their surplus cash.

One of the primary features of liquid funds is their liquidity. Investors can typically redeem their investments quickly, often within one business day. This makes liquid funds an ideal choice for individuals looking to maintain an emergency fund or for those who want to earn better returns on their idle cash compared to traditional savings accounts. Furthermore, the withdrawal process is straightforward, providing investors with access to their money without incurring significant penalties or fees.

Liquid funds also offer relatively low risk. Since these funds invest in high-quality debt instruments, the probability of default is minimal. The underlying assets are generally issued by reputable entities, such as government institutions and large corporations, which further enhances the safety of the investment. Retail investors can feel secure knowing that their capital is largely protected while still earning a return that is typically higher than that of a savings account or fixed deposit.

In terms of returns, liquid funds may provide better yields than traditional fixed-income options. While the returns can fluctuate due to changes in interest rates and market conditions, they usually range from 3% to 7% annually. This makes liquid funds a suitable option for conservative investors who are looking to achieve some growth without taking on excessive risk. Additionally, the returns from liquid funds are generally tax-efficient, as they are treated as short-term capital gains when held for less than three years, which can be beneficial for investors in higher tax brackets.

Investing in liquid funds can also be a strategic move for those looking to allocate their assets efficiently. Retail investors can use these funds as a component of a diversified portfolio, balancing their investments in equities, bonds, and other asset classes. By keeping a portion of their investments in liquid funds, investors can ensure they have readily available funds for emergencies or upcoming expenses while still taking advantage of the potential for higher returns compared to traditional cash holdings.

81. Can I lose all my money in a mutual fund?

Investing in mutual funds is often seen as a safer option compared to individual stock investments, but the question of whether you can lose all your money in a mutual fund deserves careful consideration. While mutual funds provide diversification by pooling money from many investors to invest in a broad range of securities, they are not immune to market risks. The value of your investment can fluctuate depending on the performance of the underlying assets, and in extreme cases, it is possible to face significant losses.

The risk of losing all your money in a mutual fund is largely mitigated by the nature of these investment vehicles. Mutual funds are regulated by government entities, which impose rules and standards designed to protect investors. The funds are managed by professionals who aim to maximize returns while managing risks. However, the level of risk varies from fund to fund, depending on the asset allocation strategy, investment objectives, and market conditions. Funds that invest heavily in volatile assets, such as small-cap stocks or emerging markets, may expose investors to a higher risk of loss.

In rare situations, you could experience a total loss in a mutual fund if the fund's investments become worthless. This might occur if the companies in which the fund invests go bankrupt or if there is a catastrophic market event that severely impacts the value of all securities. However, such scenarios are uncommon, and diversification within mutual funds typically provides a buffer against total loss. Most mutual funds hold a variety of assets, which helps spread out risk and reduces the likelihood of complete financial failure.

Additionally, investors should consider the impact of market conditions and their investment horizon. Mutual funds are generally not designed for short-term trading, and market fluctuations can lead to temporary declines in value. Long-term investors may ride out these fluctuations and potentially recover their investments over time. Moreover, during economic downturns, certain funds may perform poorly, but historically, markets tend to recover, and many funds have rebounded as economic conditions improve.

Ultimately, while it is theoretically possible to lose all your money in a mutual fund, the structure and management of these funds significantly reduce that risk. By choosing funds that align with your risk tolerance and investment goals, diversifying your investments, and maintaining a long-term perspective, you can better safeguard your investments against total loss. Understanding the nature of mutual funds and the risks involved will empower you to make informed decisions as a retail investor.

82. How to avoid fraud in mutual fund investments?

When investing in mutual funds, retail investors need to be vigilant to avoid falling victim to fraud. One of the most effective ways to protect oneself is through thorough research. Investors should begin by verifying the credibility of the mutual fund company. This includes checking its registration with the appropriate regulatory bodies, such as the Securities and Exchange Commission (SEC) in the United States. A legitimate fund will provide transparent information about its performance, fees, and management team. Investors should also read reviews and seek opinions from independent financial advisors to gain insights into the fund's reputation.

Another critical step in avoiding fraud is understanding the investment products being offered. Retail investors should ensure they are familiar with the types of mutual funds available, including equity, bond, and balanced funds, among others. Fraudsters often exploit investors' lack of knowledge by promoting complex or high-risk products with unrealistic promises of returns. By having a solid grasp of investment basics and the specific characteristics of each fund, investors can make informed decisions and recognize red flags that may indicate fraudulent schemes.

Transparency in communication is a hallmark of reputable mutual funds. Investors should be wary of funds that lack clear and consistent communication regarding their performance and strategies. Regular updates, performance reports, and disclosures about fees and risks are standard practices for legitimate funds. If a fund is evasive about its operations or provides vague information, it may be a sign of underlying issues. Investors should always ask questions and seek comprehensive answers before committing their money.

Additionally, investors must be cautious of unsolicited offers and pressure tactics often employed by scammers. Fraudulent schemes may involve aggressive marketing strategies, urging investors to act quickly to secure a "once-in-a-lifetime" opportunity. Retail investors should take their time when considering any investment and should never feel rushed to make a decision. Taking a step back to evaluate the offer independently can help in identifying potential fraud. It is advisable to consult with a trusted financial advisor if an offer seems too good to be true.

Finally, retail investors should monitor their investments regularly and keep track of any changes in the fund's management or investment strategy. Being proactive about one's investment portfolio can help in identifying unusual activities or discrepancies early on. If an investor notices significant changes without proper notification or transparency from the fund manager, it may warrant further investigation. By staying informed and engaged with their mutual fund investments, retail investors can significantly reduce their risk of falling prey to fraudulent schemes.

83. How do market conditions affect mutual funds?

Market conditions play a crucial role in the performance of mutual funds, significantly influencing their returns, volatility, and overall strategy. Generally, market conditions can be categorized into bull markets, bear markets, and sideways or stagnant markets. Each of these conditions presents unique challenges and opportunities for mutual fund managers, who must navigate these environments to maximize returns for their investors. Understanding how these market conditions impact mutual funds can help retail investors make informed decisions about where to allocate their assets.

In a bull market, characterized by rising stock prices and investor optimism, equity mutual funds often perform exceptionally well. Fund managers may take advantage of the upward momentum by increasing their exposure to growth stocks, which typically outperform their value counterparts during this phase. As investor confidence grows, inflows into mutual funds tend to rise, further bolstering fund performance. However, even in a bull market, the strategies employed by individual funds can vary greatly, with some focusing on aggressive growth while others may prioritize steady income through dividends.

Conversely, bear markets, marked by declining prices and widespread pessimism, can present significant challenges for mutual funds. During these periods, many equity funds may experience negative returns, prompting investors to withdraw their capital. Fund managers often shift their strategies to mitigate losses, which may include increasing exposure to defensive sectors such as utilities or consumer staples that tend to be more resilient in downturns. Additionally, some funds may pivot towards fixed-income investments, such as bonds, to provide stability and income during turbulent times. Understanding these shifts is essential for retail investors looking to navigate the complexities of market conditions.

Sideways markets, where prices move within a narrow range without clear upward or downward trends, can also affect mutual fund performance. In such environments, fund managers may struggle to generate significant returns, as both stocks and bonds can exhibit limited price movement. This scenario often leads to increased volatility, making it essential for investors to remain patient and focused on their long-term goals. Mutual funds that employ active management strategies may attempt to capitalize on short-term fluctuations, but the effectiveness of this approach can vary widely.

Retail investors should also consider the impact of external factors on mutual fund performance during different market conditions. Economic indicators, interest rates, inflation, and geopolitical events can all influence market sentiment and, subsequently, the performance of mutual funds. By staying informed about these factors and how they relate to market conditions, investors can better understand the risks and potential rewards associated with their mutual fund investments. Ultimately, recognizing how market conditions affect mutual funds is a vital part of making sound investment decisions and achieving long-term financial goals.

84. Are mutual funds good for emergency funds?

When considering whether mutual funds are a suitable option for emergency funds, it's essential to understand the primary purpose of an emergency fund. An emergency fund is designed to provide quick access to cash in times of unexpected financial needs, such as medical emergencies, job loss, or urgent home repairs. Therefore, the characteristics of an ideal emergency fund include liquidity, stability, and minimal risk. While mutual funds can offer some of these features, they may not be the best fit for this specific financial goal.

One of the main advantages of mutual funds is their potential for higher returns compared to traditional savings accounts or money market accounts. However, this potential comes with increased risk and volatility. The value of mutual fund investments can fluctuate based on market conditions, which means that during a time of financial emergency, investors might find their funds have decreased in value. This unpredictability can be particularly concerning when you need immediate access to cash, as you could end up selling your mutual fund shares at a loss.

Liquidity is another critical consideration. While many mutual funds allow investors to redeem their shares relatively quickly, the process is not instantaneous. It typically takes a few days for the transaction to be processed, which may not align with the urgency required in an emergency situation. In contrast, a dedicated emergency fund held in a high-yield savings account offers the advantage of immediate access to cash without the risk of market fluctuations.

Moreover, mutual funds often come with fees, including management fees and potential load fees, which can erode returns over time. For an emergency fund, where the aim is to preserve capital rather than grow it, the costs associated with mutual funds can diminish the safety net you are trying to establish. Retail investors should weigh these costs against the need for quick access to their funds during emergencies.

Ultimately, while mutual funds can be beneficial for long-term investment goals, they may not be the most appropriate choice for emergency savings. Retail investors are advised to prioritize liquidity and stability when setting aside funds for emergencies. Alternatives such as high-yield savings accounts or certificates of deposit (CDs) can provide a safer and more accessible option for preserving capital while still offering some growth potential.

85. Can I hold mutual funds jointly with someone?

Yes, you can hold mutual funds jointly with someone else. This arrangement is commonly seen among family members, friends, or partners who wish to invest together. Joint ownership of mutual fund accounts allows for shared investment goals and the pooling of resources, which can be especially beneficial for smaller investors seeking to diversify their portfolios. However, it is essential to understand the implications and responsibilities that come with joint ownership.

When you hold mutual funds jointly, both account holders have equal rights to the investment. This means that both parties can make decisions regarding the account, including buying or selling shares, changing investment strategies, or withdrawing funds. It is crucial for both investors to communicate openly about their investment objectives and preferences to avoid potential conflicts. Establishing clear guidelines on how to manage the account can help ensure a smooth investment experience for both parties.

There are two primary ways to hold mutual funds jointly: as joint tenants with rights of survivorship (JTWROS) or as tenants in common (TIC). JTWROS means that if one account holder passes away, the surviving owner automatically inherits the entire account. This arrangement can simplify the transfer of assets and avoid probate. On the other hand, TIC allows for each owner's share of the account to be passed on according to their will or estate plan. Understanding these differences is vital when deciding how to structure joint ownership.

Before investing in mutual funds jointly, consider the tax implications and how they may affect both account holders. Any dividends, interest, or capital gains generated by the mutual fund will be reported to the IRS, and both parties will need to account for their share of the income on their tax returns. Additionally, the financial situation of each investor could influence the overall tax burden. Therefore, it is advisable to consult with a tax professional to ensure that both parties understand their responsibilities and potential liabilities.

In conclusion, holding mutual funds jointly can be a strategic way to invest collaboratively, but it requires careful consideration and planning. Both parties should be aligned in their investment goals and maintain open communication throughout the investment process. By understanding the different ownership structures and tax implications, investors can make informed decisions that benefit both parties. Ultimately, a well-managed joint investment account can lead to shared financial success and help achieve common financial objectives.

86. What is the ideal time horizon for mutual funds?

The ideal time horizon for mutual funds largely depends on an investor's financial goals, risk tolerance, and investment strategy. Generally, a time horizon refers to the duration an investor plans to hold an investment before needing to access the funds. For mutual funds, this can range from short-term to long-term, and understanding this concept is crucial for making informed investment decisions.

Short-term time horizons, typically spanning less than three years, are suited for investors who may need their money soon, such as for a major purchase or an emergency fund. In this scenario, investors might lean toward conservative mutual funds, such as money market funds or bond funds, which offer stability and liquidity. However, these funds may provide lower returns compared to equity funds. Therefore, while short-term investments can safeguard against market volatility, they might not fully capitalize on the potential growth of the market.

On the other hand, long-term time horizons, usually defined as five years or more, allow investors to withstand market fluctuations and benefit from the compounding effect. Investors targeting retirement, children's education, or wealth accumulation often fall into this category. Equity mutual funds and growth-oriented funds are typically recommended for these investors, as they historically have delivered higher returns over extended periods. The key is to remain patient and avoid reacting to short-term market movements, as long-term investing can substantially enhance overall portfolio performance.

A medium-term horizon, ranging from three to five years, often requires a balanced approach. Investors may choose a mix of equity and fixed-income mutual funds to achieve a blend of growth and stability. This strategy can help mitigate risks while still providing decent returns. It is essential for investors to assess their individual financial situations and market conditions to determine the right balance of risk and reward for their medium-term investments.

Ultimately, the ideal time horizon for mutual funds is a personal decision influenced by various factors, including individual financial goals and market outlook. Retail investors should carefully evaluate their circumstances and consult financial professionals if needed. By aligning their investment choices with their time horizon, investors can enhance their chances of achieving financial success and navigating the complexities of the mutual fund landscape effectively.

87. How to set realistic investment goals?

Setting realistic investment goals is a crucial step for retail investors looking to navigate the complexities of mutual funds. The first step in establishing these goals is to assess your financial situation. Consider your current income, expenses, savings, and debts. Understanding your financial landscape will help you determine how much you can realistically invest over a certain period. It's also important to evaluate your risk tolerance, which varies from person to person. Knowing whether you are comfortable with high-risk investments or prefer a more conservative approach will shape your investment strategy significantly.

Once you have a clear picture of your finances and risk tolerance, the next step is to define your investment objectives. These objectives should be specific, measurable, achievable, relevant, and time-bound (SMART). For example, instead of setting a vague goal like "I want to save for retirement," you might specify, "I want to accumulate $500,000 in my retirement fund in 20 years." This level of clarity helps you stay focused and allows for better tracking of your progress. It's essential to align your goals with significant life milestones, such as buying a home, funding education, or planning for retirement.

After defining your goals, consider the time horizon for each investment. Short-term goals might include saving for a vacation or a new car, while long-term goals could revolve around retirement or children's education. Different time frames require different strategies. For short-term goals, you may want to choose more liquid investments that can be accessed quickly. In contrast, long-term goals can benefit from investments with higher potential returns, such as equity mutual funds, despite their inherent volatility. Understanding the importance of time in your investment strategy can significantly enhance your chances of achieving your objectives.

Next, regularly reviewing and adjusting your investment goals is essential as your financial situation and market conditions change. Life events such as marriage, the birth of a child, or changes in employment can impact your financial priorities and available resources. Furthermore, market fluctuations can influence the performance of your investments, which may necessitate a reevaluation of your goals. Establishing a routine for reviewing your investment progress—at least annually—will help you stay on track and make informed adjustments when necessary.

Lastly, it's vital to remain patient and disciplined throughout your investment journey. Achieving realistic investment goals often takes time, and the market can be unpredictable. Avoid the temptation to react impulsively to market volatility, as this can derail your long-term plans. Instead, focus on your established goals and trust the process. Consistent contributions to your investments, along with a well-thought-out strategy, will ultimately lead to the desired outcomes. By staying committed to your investment plan and maintaining a long-term perspective, you can effectively work towards achieving your financial objectives.

88. What are the red flags to avoid in a mutual fund?

When investing in mutual funds, it's crucial to be aware of certain red flags that can indicate potential problems with a fund. The first major red flag to watch for is a history of poor performance. While past performance is not indicative of future results, a consistent trend of underperforming its benchmark or peer group may suggest underlying issues with the fund's management or strategy. Investors should analyze performance over various time frames, including one, three, and five years, to get a comprehensive view of the fund's track record.

Another warning sign is excessive fees and expenses, which can significantly erode returns over time. Retail investors should closely examine the fund's expense ratio, as well as any sales loads or redemption fees that may apply. High fees can be a red flag, especially if they do not correlate with higher performance. Investors should seek funds that offer a good balance between fees and investment returns, ensuring they are not overpaying for mediocre performance.

Frequent changes in the fund's management team can also be a red flag. A stable management team usually indicates a coherent investment strategy and a commitment to the fund's success. Conversely, regular turnover in management can signal instability and may lead to inconsistent investment decisions. Before investing, retail investors should research the fund's management history and consider the implications of any recent changes in leadership.

Additionally, a lack of transparency regarding the fund's holdings and strategy is concerning. Mutual funds are required to disclose their holdings periodically, and investors should be wary of funds that do not provide this information or offer vague descriptions of their investment strategy. Transparency is essential for understanding how a fund operates and ensuring it aligns with an investor's goals and risk tolerance. If a fund is reticent about its investments, it may indicate a lack of accountability or a strategy that could be risky.

Finally, investors should be cautious of funds that heavily promote themselves through aggressive marketing tactics. While marketing is a natural part of the investment landscape, an overemphasis on flashy advertising rather than performance or strategy can be a red flag. Retail investors should focus on the fundamentals of the fund, such as its investment philosophy, historical performance, and risk profile, rather than being swayed by catchy slogans or promotions. By remaining vigilant and informed, investors can navigate the mutual fund landscape more effectively and avoid potentially detrimental choices.

89. Should I consider global mutual funds?

Investing in global mutual funds can be an appealing option for retail investors looking to diversify their portfolios beyond domestic markets. Global mutual funds invest in securities from various countries, allowing investors to gain exposure to international economies and industries. This diversification can potentially reduce risk, as different markets often do not move in tandem. For instance, while one country might be experiencing economic growth, another could be facing a downturn. By spreading investments across multiple regions, investors may enhance their chances of achieving more stable returns.

One key consideration when evaluating global mutual funds is the level of risk associated with investing in foreign markets. Global funds can be subject to currency fluctuations, political instability, and economic changes in the countries where they invest. These factors can impact the performance of the fund, sometimes leading to greater volatility compared to domestic mutual funds. Therefore, retail investors should assess their risk tolerance and investment goals before committing to a global fund. Understanding the specific regions or countries the fund targets can also provide insight into potential risks and rewards.

Another important aspect of global mutual funds is their potential for higher returns. Emerging markets, for instance, may offer growth opportunities that are not available in developed markets. Investing in these regions can yield significant gains if the economies continue to expand. However, retail investors must conduct thorough research to identify funds with strong management teams and solid track records in international investing. Evaluating the fund's historical performance, expense ratios, and investment strategy can help investors make informed decisions.

In addition to growth potential, global mutual funds can be an effective tool for asset allocation. By including international investments in a portfolio, investors can achieve a more balanced allocation across different asset classes and geographical locations. This diversification can provide protection against domestic economic downturns and enhance overall portfolio performance. Retail investors should consider how global mutual funds fit into their broader investment strategy and whether they complement other holdings in their portfolios.

Ultimately, the decision to invest in global mutual funds should be based on individual financial goals, risk tolerance, and investment horizon. Retail investors are encouraged to consult with financial advisors or conduct their own research to determine if these funds align with their overall investment strategy. By weighing the benefits and risks associated with global mutual funds, investors can make informed choices that may lead to a more diversified and potentially lucrative investment portfolio.

90. How do I stay updated on mutual fund trends?

Staying updated on mutual fund trends is essential for retail investors who want to make informed decisions about their investments. One of the most effective ways to keep track of these trends is through financial news outlets and investment websites that specialize in mutual funds. Publications like Bloomberg, Morningstar, and The Wall Street Journal often provide insights into market developments, fund performances, and broader economic indicators that can affect mutual funds. Subscribing to newsletters or alerts from these sources can ensure you receive timely updates directly in your inbox.

Another valuable resource for tracking mutual fund trends is the Financial Industry Regulatory Authority (FINRA) and the Securities and Exchange Commission (SEC). These regulatory bodies offer educational materials and updates about mutual funds, including changes in regulations, compliance requirements, and investor protection measures. By familiarizing yourself with the resources available on their websites, you can gain a deeper understanding of the market landscape and how it can impact your investment choices.

Engaging with investment communities, whether online or in-person, can also provide valuable insights into mutual fund trends. Discussion forums, social media groups, and local investment clubs allow retail investors to share experiences, strategies, and news about various funds. These platforms can serve as a space for asking questions and gaining diverse perspectives, helping you stay informed about the latest trends and fund performance in a collaborative environment.

Utilizing financial tools and apps designed for investors is another effective way to monitor mutual fund trends. Many platforms offer real-time data, portfolio tracking, and analysis tools that can help you stay on top of market shifts.

By setting up alerts for specific funds or market conditions, you can receive notifications that allow you to react quickly to changes, ensuring you remain proactive in your investment strategy.

Lastly, consider following industry experts and analysts on social media or through their blogs and podcasts. Many financial professionals share their insights and analyses on current trends in mutual funds, often breaking down complex information into digestible formats. By following these experts, you can access a wealth of knowledge that not only keeps you updated on trends but also enhances your overall understanding of mutual fund investing.

91. How to use mutual funds for long-term wealth creation?

Mutual funds are a popular investment vehicle for retail investors seeking long-term wealth creation due to their professional management, diversification, and accessibility. To effectively use mutual funds for wealth creation, investors should first understand their financial goals and risk tolerance. Setting clear objectives, such as saving for retirement, a child's education, or a major purchase, helps in selecting the right mutual fund types that align with these goals. For instance, equity funds may be suitable for those with a higher risk appetite looking for growth over an extended period, while balanced funds may appeal to more conservative investors seeking a mix of income and capital appreciation.

Once the investment goals are established, investors should focus on selecting the appropriate mutual funds. It is crucial to conduct thorough research on various funds available in the market. This involves analyzing performance history, fund manager expertise, expense ratios, and the underlying assets of the fund. Investors should consider funds that have consistently outperformed their benchmarks over a significant period, as this can be an indicator of effective management and sound investment strategies. Additionally, understanding the fund's investment style—whether it is actively managed or passively tracks an index—can also influence long-term performance.

Investors should adopt a disciplined investment strategy when using mutual funds for wealth creation. This includes regular investments through systematic investment plans (SIPs), which allow for investing a fixed amount at regular intervals. SIPs help in averaging out the cost of investment and reduce the impact of market volatility. By maintaining a consistent investment approach, investors can benefit from the power of compounding, which can significantly enhance wealth over time. Moreover, staying invested for the long term reduces the temptation to react to short-term market fluctuations.

Monitoring the performance of mutual funds is essential, but it should be done with a long-term perspective. Investors should review their portfolios periodically to ensure that their chosen funds continue to align with their financial goals and risk tolerance. While it is important to keep an eye on performance, it is equally crucial to avoid making impulsive decisions based on market noise or short-term performance dips. A well-structured investment plan should account for periodic rebalancing, which may involve adjusting the allocation among different funds to maintain the desired risk profile.

Lastly, understanding the tax implications of mutual fund investments is vital for long-term wealth creation. Retail investors should be aware of the tax treatment of capital gains and dividends associated with mutual funds. For instance, holding equity mutual funds for more than one year typically qualifies for long-term capital gains tax, which is often lower than short-term capital gains tax. By strategically selecting funds and planning the duration of the investment, investors can optimize their after-tax returns. Overall, using mutual funds wisely can be a powerful strategy for achieving long-term financial goals and building wealth.

92. What are the benefits of compounding in mutual funds?

Compounding is a powerful concept in finance, especially in the context of mutual funds. It refers to the process where the returns on an investment generate additional returns over time. When investors put their money into mutual funds, they not only benefit from the growth of their initial capital but also from the growth of any returns that are reinvested. This creates a snowball effect, where the investment grows exponentially, particularly over long periods. Retail investors can harness this effect to significantly enhance their wealth accumulation.

One of the primary benefits of compounding in mutual funds is the potential for exponential growth. When investors reinvest dividends and capital gains back into the fund, they increase the total investment base. This larger base can then earn more returns, which can be reinvested again, leading to a cycle of growth. For example, if an investor's mutual fund generates a 10% annual return and they reinvest those earnings, the following year's returns will be calculated on a higher principal amount, thus amplifying the growth potential.

Another important aspect of compounding is the time factor. The earlier an investor starts investing in mutual funds, the more they can benefit from compounding. This is often illustrated through the concept of "time in the market" rather than "timing the market." Even small amounts invested early can grow substantially due to the time available for compounding to take effect. Retail investors who adopt a long-term investment strategy can see their investments mature significantly, thanks to the compounding effect.

Moreover, mutual funds often have the advantage of professional management, which can enhance compounding potential. Fund managers use their expertise to select investments that are likely to perform well over time. By choosing funds that align with long-term growth strategies, investors can benefit from both compounding and the strategic asset allocation conducted by professionals. This adds an additional layer of potential growth, as skilled fund managers can identify opportunities that may outperform general market returns.

Lastly, compounding can also provide a hedge against inflation. As the cost of living rises, the purchasing power of money decreases. However, by investing in mutual funds that compound over time, investors can potentially achieve returns that outpace inflation. This means that the real value of their investments can grow, providing not only financial security but also the opportunity to meet future needs and goals. For retail investors, understanding and leveraging the benefits of compounding in mutual funds can be a key strategy for building wealth over the long term.

93. How to create a balanced mutual fund portfolio?

Creating a balanced mutual fund portfolio involves a strategic approach that aligns with your financial goals, risk tolerance, and investment horizon. The first step is to assess your individual investment objectives. Are you looking for long-term growth, income through dividends, or a combination of both? Understanding your primary goals will guide you in selecting the types of mutual funds that best fit your needs. For instance, if you aim for long-term growth, equity funds may be more suitable, whereas if you require regular income, bond or income funds might be preferable.

Next, consider the importance of diversification within your portfolio. A well-diversified portfolio can help mitigate risk by spreading investments across various asset classes, sectors, and geographical regions. This means not putting all your money into one type of fund. A balanced portfolio may include a mix of equity funds, bond funds, and perhaps some international funds to capture global opportunities. By diversifying, you can reduce the impact of poor performance in any single investment, as gains in other areas can offset losses.

Determining your risk tolerance is crucial when creating a balanced mutual fund portfolio. Risk tolerance varies among investors based on factors like age, income, and financial stability. Generally, younger investors may afford to take on more risk due to a longer investment horizon, while those closer to retirement might prefer more conservative investments. Assessing your risk tolerance helps in deciding the ratio of equity to bond funds. A common approach is the rule of 100, which suggests subtracting your age from 100 to determine the percentage of your portfolio that should be invested in equities.

Regularly reviewing and rebalancing your portfolio is essential to maintain your desired asset allocation. Market fluctuations can cause your investments to drift away from your original targets. For instance, if equity funds outperform bond funds, your portfolio may become overly weighted in equities, increasing your risk exposure. Setting a schedule for periodic reviews, such as annually or semi-annually, allows you to assess performance and make necessary adjustments to realign with your investment strategy and risk tolerance.

Finally, consider the costs associated with the mutual funds in your portfolio. Expense ratios, transaction fees, and management fees can significantly impact your overall returns. When selecting mutual funds, it's important to compare these costs and consider their implications on your long-term investment performance. Opting for low-cost index funds or exchange-traded funds (ETFs) can be a smart way to reduce expenses while still achieving diversification. By keeping an eye on costs and ensuring you have a balanced mix of investments, you can enhance your chances of reaching your financial objectives effectively.

94. What are the best practices for SIP investments?

Investing in Systematic Investment Plans (SIPs) can be a rewarding strategy for retail investors looking to build wealth over time. Understanding the best practices for SIP investments is essential to maximize potential returns while managing risks effectively. The first best practice is to start early. The power of compounding works best when investors give their money more time to grow. By starting early, even small amounts can accumulate significantly over the years, making a substantial difference in the final corpus.

Another critical practice is to have a clear investment goal. Whether the aim is saving for retirement, funding children's education, or purchasing a home, having specific financial objectives can guide investment choices. Investors should align their SIPs with the time horizon of their goals, selecting funds that match their risk tolerance and expected returns. This clarity not only helps in choosing the right mutual funds but also in maintaining discipline during market fluctuations.

Diversification is also a cornerstone of effective SIP investment. Retail investors should consider spreading their investments across different mutual funds that focus on various asset classes, such as equity, debt, and hybrid funds. This strategy reduces risk, as different asset classes often perform differently under varying market conditions. By diversifying within their SIPs, investors can cushion themselves against significant losses while still participating in market gains.

Regular monitoring of SIP investments is vital to ensure they remain aligned with financial goals. Investors should review their portfolios periodically, assessing the performance of the funds and making adjustments if necessary. Market conditions, changes in personal circumstances, or shifts in investment objectives can all warrant a reevaluation. However, it's important to avoid making impulsive decisions based on short-term market movements; instead, focus on long-term performance trends.

Lastly, maintaining a disciplined approach is fundamental to the success of SIP investments. This means continuing contributions regardless of market conditions and resisting the urge to time the market. Investors should adhere to their investment plans, even during market downturns, as consistent investing can lead to lower average costs per unit over time. By fostering a disciplined mindset, retail investors can enhance their chances of achieving their long-term financial goals through SIPs.

95. How to manage market volatility as a mutual fund investor?

Market volatility can be a significant concern for mutual fund investors, as it often leads to fluctuations in fund performance and investor anxiety. Understanding how to manage this volatility is crucial for maintaining a long-term investment strategy. One of the first steps in managing market volatility is to adopt a long-term perspective. By focusing on long-term goals rather than short-term market movements, investors can reduce the emotional stress associated with daily market fluctuations. A well-structured investment plan that aligns with individual financial objectives will help keep investors grounded during turbulent times.

Diversification is another essential strategy for managing market volatility. By investing in a variety of asset classes, sectors, and geographical regions, mutual fund investors can spread their risk. A diversified portfolio can help cushion the impact of market downturns, as not all investments will respond the same way to economic changes. When selecting mutual funds, consider those that offer a mix of equity, fixed income, and alternative investments. This approach can lead to a more stable overall portfolio performance, even when specific sectors experience volatility.

Regular portfolio review and rebalancing are vital components of managing volatility. Over time, certain investments may grow faster than others, leading to an unbalanced portfolio that may not align with an investor's risk tolerance or objectives. By routinely reviewing and rebalancing the portfolio, investors can ensure that they are maintaining their desired level of risk exposure. This practice not only helps in managing volatility but also promotes disciplined investing, as it encourages a systematic approach to buying low and selling high.

Investors should also be mindful of their emotional responses during periods of market volatility. Fear and greed can prompt impulsive decisions that may not align with an investor's long-term strategy. It is essential for mutual fund investors to stay informed about market trends and economic indicators while resisting the urge to react hastily to short-term changes. Utilizing tools such as dollar-cost averaging can also help mitigate the impact of volatility by allowing investors to purchase more shares when prices are low and fewer shares when prices are high.

Finally, consider seeking professional advice when navigating market volatility. Financial advisors can provide valuable insights and help investors develop strategies tailored to their individual circumstances. They can also offer guidance on the selection of mutual funds that align with an investor's risk tolerance and investment goals. Engaging with a professional can enhance an investor's confidence and provide a sense of security during uncertain market conditions, ultimately leading to more informed and effective investment decisions.

Conclusion

96. What are the key takeaways from this book?

One of the key takeaways from "Investing Simplified: 101 Answers About Mutual Funds" is the importance of understanding mutual funds as a fundamental investment vehicle. Retail investors often encounter a complex landscape of financial products, but mutual funds stand out due to their diversification, professional management, and accessibility. This book emphasizes that mutual funds allow investors to pool their money with others, which helps spread risk across a variety of securities. A clear grasp of how mutual funds operate can empower investors to make informed decisions tailored to their financial goals.

Another significant takeaway is the need to assess risk tolerance and investment objectives before selecting mutual funds. The book guides readers through the process of determining their risk appetite, which can differ widely among individuals. By understanding personal financial goals—whether they are saving for retirement, funding education, or building wealth—investors can choose mutual funds that align with their desired outcomes. This alignment is crucial for maintaining a consistent investment strategy over time, minimizing emotional decision-making during market fluctuations.

The book also highlights the importance of evaluating mutual fund performance metrics. Retail investors are equipped with the knowledge to analyze key indicators such as expense ratios, historical returns, and fund manager performance. By understanding these metrics, investors can make comparisons between different funds and select those that not only have a solid track record but also fit within their investment philosophy. This analytical approach is essential for navigating the often overwhelming array of mutual fund options available in the market.

Additionally, the text stresses the significance of ongoing education and staying informed about market trends. The investment landscape is dynamic and can be influenced by various economic factors. Retail investors are encouraged to continually educate themselves about market developments, regulatory changes, and emerging investment strategies. By doing so, they can adapt their portfolios as needed and seize new opportunities that may arise, making informed adjustments in line with their long-term financial goals.

Finally, the book underscores the value of patience and discipline in investing. Many retail investors may be tempted to react impulsively to market volatility, but the principles outlined in "Investing Simplified" advocate for a steady, long-term approach. By sticking to a well-thought-out investment plan and resisting the urge to make knee-jerk reactions, investors can enhance their chances of achieving their financial objectives. This emphasis on patience serves as a reminder that successful investing is often a marathon, not a sprint, and that the right mindset can significantly impact investment outcomes.

97. How to stay disciplined as a mutual fund investor?

Staying disciplined as a mutual fund investor is crucial for achieving long-term financial goals. The financial markets can be volatile, and the emotional responses to market fluctuations can lead to poor decision-making. To maintain discipline, investors should establish clear investment goals and a strategy that aligns with those goals. This involves determining risk tolerance, investment horizon, and financial objectives before making any investment decisions. By having a well-defined plan, investors can navigate market ups and downs without deviating from their intended path.

Another essential aspect of discipline is adhering to a consistent investment schedule. Regular contributions to mutual funds, whether through systematic investment plans (SIPs) or lump-sum investments, help cultivate a habit of investing. This approach not only averages out the cost of investment over time but also encourages investors to treat investing as a priority rather than an afterthought. By committing to a disciplined investment routine, investors can mitigate the temptation to react impulsively to market changes.

Monitoring investments is important, but excessive scrutiny can lead to anxiety and rash decisions. Retail investors should aim for a balance between staying informed and avoiding overreaction to short-term market movements. Setting specific intervals for portfolio reviews, such as quarterly or annually, can help investors stay on track without becoming overly focused on daily market fluctuations. During these reviews, it is important to assess performance against benchmarks and determine whether the mutual funds still align with the investor's long-term goals.

Emotional resilience is another vital component of discipline in investing. Market downturns can trigger fear, prompting investors to sell at a loss or shift to less suitable investments. To counter this, investors should remind themselves of their initial objectives and the reasons behind their investment choices. Developing a mindset that embraces a long-term perspective can help investors remain calm during turbulent times. Techniques such as mindfulness or consulting with a financial advisor can aid in maintaining a balanced emotional state.

Finally, education plays a key role in fostering discipline. Retail investors should continuously seek to enhance their understanding of mutual funds and market dynamics. By staying informed about market trends, investment strategies, and economic indicators, investors can make more informed decisions and remain committed to their investment plans. Joining investment clubs, attending seminars, or reading relevant literature can provide valuable insights and reinforce the importance of disciplined investing. Ultimately, a disciplined approach not only helps investors weather market volatility but also positions them for long-term financial success.

98. Why should you seek professional advice when needed?

Seeking professional advice when investing in mutual funds can significantly enhance your decision-making process. Retail investors often face a plethora of choices that can be overwhelming. Professional advisors possess the expertise and insights necessary to navigate the complexities of the financial markets. They can provide tailored recommendations based on your individual financial situation, risk tolerance, and investment goals. This personalized approach ensures that your investment strategy is aligned with your overarching financial objectives.

One of the primary reasons to consult with a financial advisor is access to a wealth of knowledge. Professionals in the field stay updated on market trends, regulatory changes, and emerging investment opportunities. They have the tools and resources to analyze various mutual fund options meticulously. This depth of knowledge allows them to identify funds that have the potential for strong performance while mitigating risks. Retail investors might miss critical details or nuances that could affect their investment outcomes, making professional guidance invaluable.

Moreover, professional advisors can help you create a diversified investment portfolio. Diversification is a fundamental principle of investing that can reduce risk by spreading investments across various asset classes and sectors. A financial advisor can assess your current holdings and recommend adjustments to optimize diversification. This approach not only helps protect your investments during market volatility but also positions you for potential growth. Retail investors may lack the experience to effectively balance their portfolios, making professional advice essential.

In addition to providing investment strategies, financial advisors can assist with behavioral aspects of investing. Emotional decision-making can lead to poor investment choices, such as panic selling during market downturns or chasing after high-performing funds without proper analysis. Advisors offer objective perspectives and can help you stick to a disciplined investment plan. This guidance is crucial for maintaining focus on long-term goals rather than succumbing to short-term market fluctuations, which often derail retail investors.

Finally, professional advice can save you time and effort. Conducting thorough research on mutual funds and keeping up with market developments demands significant time and expertise. By working with a financial advisor, retail investors can delegate these tasks and focus on other priorities in their lives. This partnership not only streamlines the investment process but also provides peace of mind, knowing that your investments are being managed by a knowledgeable professional. Ultimately, seeking professional advice can lead to more informed decisions and better investment outcomes for retail investors in the mutual fund space.

99. What additional resources can help in mutual fund investing?

Investing in mutual funds can be a rewarding venture, but it often requires additional resources to enhance understanding and improve investment strategies. Retail investors can benefit greatly from a variety of tools and platforms that provide insights, research, and education. One key resource is online financial news websites, which offer up-to-date information on market trends and specific mutual fund performance. Websites like Morningstar, Yahoo Finance, and Bloomberg can help investors compare funds, analyze their historical performance, and read expert opinions. These platforms often feature valuable articles and analysis that can deepen an investor's understanding of market dynamics.

Another vital resource for mutual fund investors is educational content provided by financial institutions and investment firms. Many mutual fund companies offer webinars, podcasts, and online courses that cover the basics of mutual fund investing, portfolio management, and market analysis. Retail investors can take advantage of these materials to build their knowledge and confidence in making informed investment decisions. Additionally, financial advisors can serve as a significant resource. While not every investor may choose to work with a professional, consulting with a financial advisor can provide personalized advice tailored to individual investment goals and risk tolerance.

Investment apps have also emerged as powerful tools for retail investors. These apps often provide features that enable users to track their investments, analyze performance, and receive alerts on market changes. Many investment platforms include educational resources directly within the app, making it easier for investors to learn on-the-go. Features such as virtual trading allow investors to practice their strategies without risking real money, which can be particularly beneficial for beginners. Understanding how to use these apps effectively can empower retail investors to make better decisions.

Books and online forums dedicated to investing can further supplement knowledge. Reading books written by experienced investors and financial experts can provide deeper insights into investment strategies and market psychology. Forums and communities, such as those found on platforms like Reddit or investment-focused websites, allow investors to share experiences, ask questions, and learn from one another. Engaging in discussions with peers can lead to valuable insights that may not be readily available through traditional educational resources.

Finally, government and regulatory websites should not be overlooked as important resources. The Securities and Exchange Commission (SEC) and the Financial Industry Regulatory Authority (FINRA) provide extensive information on mutual fund regulations, investor rights, and educational materials regarding investment practices. Retail investors can access vital information on how to recognize fraudulent schemes and understand their rights as investors. By leveraging these various resources, retail investors can enhance their knowledge and make informed decisions in their mutual fund investing journey.

100. How to ensure financial independence using mutual funds?

Achieving financial independence is a goal for many retail investors, and mutual funds can serve as a valuable tool in this pursuit. To ensure financial independence using mutual funds, it is essential to understand the various types of mutual funds available and how they can fit into a broader investment strategy. Equity funds, bond funds, index funds, and balanced funds each offer different risk and return profiles, allowing investors to diversify their portfolios according to their risk tolerance and investment horizon.

One of the key steps to achieving financial independence through mutual funds is to set clear financial goals. Investors should determine what financial independence means for them—whether it is retiring early, funding education, or achieving a certain lifestyle. By setting specific, measurable, achievable, relevant, and time-bound (SMART) goals, investors can create a roadmap for their investments. This clarity can help in selecting the right mutual funds that align with these goals, ensuring that investment choices support long-term aspirations.

Another crucial aspect is to regularly invest through systematic investment plans (SIPs). SIPs allow investors to contribute fixed amounts to mutual funds at regular intervals, which can help in averaging the cost of investment and mitigating market volatility. This disciplined approach not only fosters a habit of saving but also benefits from the power of compounding. Over time, the cumulative effect of consistent investments can significantly enhance the potential for wealth accumulation, ultimately contributing to financial independence.

Monitoring and rebalancing the investment portfolio is equally important. As markets fluctuate and personal circumstances change, the initial asset allocation may shift. Regularly reviewing mutual fund performance and the overall portfolio can help investors identify underperforming funds and make necessary adjustments. Rebalancing ensures that the portfolio remains aligned with the investor's risk tolerance and financial goals, making it a dynamic strategy for maintaining a path toward financial independence.

Lastly, educating oneself about mutual funds and investment strategies is vital for informed decision-making. Retail investors should take the initiative to understand the fees associated with mutual funds, tax implications, and the importance of diversification. Participating in investment workshops, reading financial literature, or consulting with financial advisors can enhance investment knowledge. By being well-informed, investors can navigate the complexities of mutual funds effectively, increasing their chances of achieving financial independence over time.

101. Why is understanding mutual funds a lifelong skill?

Understanding mutual funds is a lifelong skill for retail investors because these investment vehicles serve as a cornerstone for building wealth over time. Mutual funds allow individuals to pool their resources with others, gaining access to diversified portfolios managed by professionals. This collective approach reduces risk and enhances the potential for returns, making mutual funds an appealing option for both novice and seasoned investors. As the financial landscape continues to evolve, grasping the nuances of mutual funds becomes essential for making informed investment decisions.

The dynamic nature of mutual funds demands investors stay informed about various types, structures, and performance metrics. Different fund categories, such as equity, fixed income, and balanced funds, cater to varying risk appetites and investment goals. Understanding these distinctions enables investors to align their choices with their financial objectives, whether that involves aggressive growth, income generation, or capital preservation. As personal circumstances and market conditions change, the ability to reassess and adapt one's mutual fund strategy is crucial for long-term success.

Moreover, the regulatory environment surrounding mutual funds can impact their performance and investor experience. Knowledge of the rules governing mutual funds, including disclosure requirements and fee structures, empowers investors to make better choices. For instance, recognizing the difference between expense ratios and management fees can significantly influence net returns. By keeping abreast of regulatory changes and trends in the mutual fund industry, investors can better navigate the complexities of fund selection and management, ultimately enhancing their investment outcomes.

In addition to understanding the mechanics of mutual funds, investors should also develop a keen awareness of market trends and economic indicators that can affect fund performance. This knowledge allows for timely adjustments to investment strategies based on prevailing conditions. Being able to interpret market signals and economic data can lead to more strategic decisions regarding fund allocations and withdrawals. As global markets fluctuate and new investment opportunities arise, the skill to analyze these factors will remain invaluable.

Lastly, the habit of continual learning and engagement with mutual funds fosters financial literacy and confidence among retail investors. Participating in discussions, attending workshops, or following industry news can enhance understanding and provide insights into effective investment strategies. This ongoing education not only improves one's ability to select suitable funds but also encourages a proactive approach to personal finance. Ultimately, mastering the intricacies of mutual funds equips investors with the tools necessary to achieve their financial goals and adapt to the ever-changing investment landscape.

Recap of Key Takeaways

In the realm of mutual funds, understanding the fundamental concepts is essential for making informed investment decisions. One key takeaway is the significance of asset allocation. Retail investors need to recognize that diversifying their investments across various asset classes—not just stocks or bonds—can help mitigate risk and enhance potential returns. By strategically balancing their portfolios, investors can better weather market volatility while pursuing their financial goals.

Another critical aspect is the importance of costs associated with mutual funds. Retail investors should pay close attention to management fees, expense ratios, and any other charges that can erode returns over time. Understanding these costs can empower investors to select funds that align with their financial objectives while maximizing their investment potential. A clear comparison of fees across similar funds can provide valuable insights and lead to better investment choices.

The role of fund performance is also a key takeaway. While past performance is not indicative of future results, it serves as a useful metric for assessing a fund's historical ability to meet its investment objectives. Retail investors should consider long-term performance trends rather than being swayed by short-term fluctuations. Evaluating performance in the context of a fund's benchmark can further aid in making informed decisions about fund selection.

Additionally, the significance of understanding the underlying investment strategy of a mutual fund cannot be overstated. Each fund has a specific investment philosophy, whether it be growth, value, or income-oriented strategies.

Retail investors should familiarize themselves with these strategies to ensure alignment with their own risk tolerance and investment goals. A clear understanding of how a fund intends to achieve its objectives can guide investors in selecting the right funds for their portfolios.

Finally, the importance of regular portfolio reviews and rebalancing emerges as a crucial takeaway. Retail investors should periodically assess their mutual fund investments to ensure they remain aligned with their financial goals and risk tolerance. Market conditions may change, affecting the performance of various asset classes. By rebalancing their portfolios, investors can maintain their desired asset allocation and stay on track toward achieving their long-term investment objectives.

Final Thoughts

In the realm of investing, mutual funds have emerged as a popular choice for retail investors seeking a simpler way to grow their wealth. As we've explored throughout this book, mutual funds offer a range of benefits, including professional management, diversification, and accessibility. These features make them especially suitable for those who may not have the time or expertise to manage their own investments actively. Understanding the fundamental principles of mutual funds empowers investors to make informed decisions that align with their financial goals.

Investors should recognize that while mutual funds can be a powerful tool, they are not without risks. Market fluctuations can impact fund performance, and fees can erode returns over time. Therefore, it is crucial for investors to conduct thorough research and evaluate each fund's objectives, historical performance, and expense ratios. By doing so, they can select funds that not only match their risk tolerance but also fit their long-term investment strategies.

Another important consideration is the role of time in investing. Mutual funds are typically designed for long-term growth rather than short-term gains. Retail investors should approach their investments with a mindset focused on the future, understanding that patience can yield significant rewards. Staying invested through market ups and downs often leads to better outcomes than attempting to time the market. This long-term perspective is essential for navigating the inevitable volatility that accompanies financial markets.

Education and continuous learning are vital components of successful investing. The landscape of mutual funds is constantly evolving, with new products and strategies emerging regularly. Retail investors should take advantage of resources such as financial news, investment seminars, and online courses to stay informed. By enhancing their knowledge about mutual funds and investment strategies, investors can adapt their approaches and make better decisions that suit their personal financial situations.

In conclusion, investing in mutual funds can be a straightforward and effective way for retail investors to participate in the financial markets. By understanding the mechanics of mutual funds, recognizing the importance of risk assessment, adopting a long-term investment strategy, and committing to ongoing education, investors can significantly increase their chances of achieving their financial objectives. As you move forward in your investment journey, remember that informed decision-making is key to navigating the complexities of mutual funds and ultimately securing your financial future.

www.ingramcontent.com/pod-product-compliance
Ingram Content Group UK Ltd.
Pitfield, Milton Keynes, MK11 3LW, UK
UKHW040038200726
13845UKWH00054B/488

9 789394 808867